BEYOND

GREG LAURIE

BEYOND

MULTNOMAH
BOOKS

BEYOND
PUBLISHED BY MULTNOMAH BOOKS
12265 Oracle Boulevard, Suite 200
Colorado Springs, Colorado 80921
A division of Random House Inc.

All Scripture quotations, unless otherwise indicated, are taken from the New King James Version®. Copyright © 1982 by Thomas Nelson Inc. Used by permission. All rights reserved. Scripture quotations marked (AMP) are taken from The Amplified® Bible. Copyright © 1954, 1958, 1962, 1964, 1965, 1987 by The Lockman Foundation. Used by permission. (www.Lock man.org). Scripture quotations marked (ESV) are taken from The Holy Bible, English Standard Version, copyright © 2001 by Crossway Bibles, a division of Good News Publishers. Used by permission. All rights reserved. Scripture quotations marked (NIV) are taken from the Holy Bible, New International Version®. NIV®. Copyright © 1973, 1978, 1984 by International Bible Society. Used by permission of Zondervan Publishing House. All rights reserved. Scripture quotations marked (NLT) are taken from the Holy Bible, New Living Translation, copyright © 1996, 2004. Used by permission of Tyndale House Publishers Inc., Wheaton, Illinois 60189. All rights reserved. Scripture quotations marked (Phillips) are taken from The New Testament in Modern English, Revised Edition © 1972 by J. B. Phillips. Copyright renewed © 1986, 1988 by Vera M. Phillips.

Italics in Scripture quotations reflect the author's added emphasis.

ISBN 978-1-59052-831-0

Library of Congress Cataloging-in-Publication Data

Laurie, Greg.
    Beyond / by Greg Laurie. — 1st ed.
      p. cm.
    Includes index.
    ISBN 978-1-59052-831-0
  1. Bible—Textbooks. 2. Bible—Criticism, interpretation, etc. I. Title.
    BS605.3.L38 2007
    242'.5—dc22

                         2007009997

Printed in the United States of America
2007—First Edition

10 9 8 7 6 5 4 3 2 1

Now all glory to God, who is able, through his mighty power at work within us, to accomplish infinitely more than we might ask or think.

EPHESIANS 3:20 NLT

Getting Started

Are you happy with the way you are right now? Or are there things in your life you would like to see dramatically altered? Are there limitations and road-blocks you would like to get beyond, especially in your relationship with God? Do you sense your need to draw closer to God?

That's what I want to help you do in this book. I want to help build you up in your relationship with God by letting you see what His Word says about the things you deal with and think about every day. Things like relationships, family issues, overcoming temptation, and enduring hardships.

OUR MANUAL FOR LIVING

As our source of God's truth, the Bible serves many purposes. As God's message of redemption, it tells how we can know Him and come into a relationship with Him. And once we've started that relationship, the Bible is also our manual for living our lives in a way that pleases God. Spending time in the Bible will prepare your heart for whatever you'll face throughout the day. It helps keep our relationship with Him healthy and strong, without breakdowns, no matter what we face.

I love electronic gadgets. I hate to read the manuals, however. And as a result, I have a lot of electronic gadgets that don't work.

Our lives can be that way. Think about how many things go wrong because we have not taken the time to follow the instructions in the manual that God has given us called the Bible. The Bible is God's Word and is to be trusted when we use it to guide our lives.

So allow this book to help you take time daily for the Word of God—

to make this a top priority in your routine—so you can discover for yourself the strength and power and encouragement that God wants to make available to you.

THIS BOOK'S SETUP

As you use this book day by day, here's what you can do in each of the daily readings:

1. After getting alone and quiet and still, read my brief comments that start each day's selection.

2. Think over the sidebar scriptures or questions that you'll see in bold type.

3. Ponder carefully the Bible verse under the heading "The Lord's Invitation to His People." Ask yourself, *What does this mean for my life?* This Bible verse will usually be a direct command from God, and labeling it here as an "invitation" doesn't mean that it's merely His suggestion. It's still a command from God, with obedience being the only worthy and proper response. But don't forget that this obedience is also your open door to a stronger relationship with God and to all the wonderful experiences that come with that. He's inviting you to go beyond your present limitations and spiritual dryness. God's commands don't always make sense to us, but it's important that we obey them whether we like them or not, whether we agree with them or not.

4. Pray. There's no need for any elaborate or religious-sounding words; just talk honestly with God. (You can use the guidelines you'll see under the heading "With God in Prayer.") Focus especially on having a grateful heart and expressing your sincere gratitude to God. (There will always be something new each day to thank Him for!)

5. As you continue in prayerful thought, consider the suggestions you'll find under the heading that starts with the words "Move Beyond" (the rest of the heading is different each day). This

suggestion will always relate to actually doing something about what God invites you to. Take seriously that God invites you to be "not a forgetful hearer but a doer" of His Word—and be excited about His promise that whoever does this "will be blessed in what he does" (James 1:25).

6. As God's Holy Spirit brings to mind further reflections, application points, and things to pray about, feel free to write these down in the space provided at the end of the daily reading. If you get in the habit of writing something down here each day, this book will become a powerful record of your spiritual journey during this season in your life, and it will always be a great personal encouragement to come back and review what God has done.

You'll find enough daily readings here to last you about six months, with readings for each weekday plus one for the weekend.

My hope is that as you make your way through these readings, you'll keep asking the Lord to show you how He wants to change your life day by day. My prayer for you is that the Holy Spirit will shine His powerful light into your heart, showing you any area that should be dealt with and filling you with hope and encouragement for a lifelong adventure of following the Lord.

The Power of Impartation

Perhaps like many other people, you make bold resolutions whenever a new year rolls around. You make plans about changes you want to experience in the coming year. But it's not long until you let go of those great resolutions.

As Christians, we're often defeated in day-to-day living because we don't truly realize how many resources God has placed in our spiritual account. A lot of times we pray, *God, help me; give me this, give me that.* Meanwhile, God is saying, *Will you please go check your account? I've deposited more than you could ever use. Check it out.*

Can you imagine a soldier trying to fight a battle with no ammunition while he's sitting on a bunker filled with thousands and thousands of rounds of ammo, more than he could use in a thousand wars? He has more than he needs right under him—while trying to fight the battle without it.

> Sin is no longer your master, for you no longer live under the **requirements** of the law. Instead, you live under the freedom of God's **grace**.… You are free from the power of sin and have become slaves of God.
>
> ROMANS 6:14, 22 NLT

The reasons for our defeats in battles with sin and temptation lie largely in our ignorance of the facts. In Jesus Christ we have the power to live a new life and to no longer be under sin's control. That power is not in imitation; the power comes from impartation. We can try our hardest to imitate Jesus and to be like Him, but we will never succeed by our own efforts. Victory comes only as He imparts His life in us through His Spirit. And we'll see how many resources He's made fully available to us through His Spirit living inside us.

God has done something for you, and now it's for you to appropriate that divine provision.

THE LORD'S INVITATION TO HIS PEOPLE

Put on the new self, created after the likeness of God in true righteousness and holiness.
EPHESIANS 4:24 ESV

WITH GOD IN PRAYER

Thank Him that in Christ Jesus you're now free from slavery to sin and that by His grace you can live in victory.

MOVE BEYOND DEFEAT

Be bold and confident in the Lord's power to help you overcome temptation and sin. In what area of life does He want you to grow today in righteousness and purity, by His power?

Your own reflections...personal application... personal prayer points...

Through the Storm

Sometimes we may think that when we're in the will of God, our lives should be smooth sailing. But many times it's just the opposite. Doors slam in our faces. Obstacles appear in our paths. Storms arise that threaten to drive us off course.

That's why we need to remember there's a devil who wants to stop us from doing what God wants us to do.

As Paul pressed forward to do the will of God, he hit some tough times. For example, while he was being taken across the sea to Rome, a massive storm arose that caused others on the ship to despair of their lives. But there was no obstacle big enough to stop Paul. He always seemed to rise above his circumstances. As he endured the storm, he knew God had shown him what to do, and he would let nothing deter him from his course.

> So take **courage**! For I believe
> God. It will be just as **he** said.
> ACTS 27:25 NLT

Often when a hard time hits, when a crisis hits, when a tragedy hits, we want out. We ask God for an airlift out of our problems. But many times God wants us to learn in the midst of those difficulties—and to learn especially about His love for us:

Can anything ever separate us from Christ's love? Does it mean he no longer loves us if we have trouble or calamity, or are persecuted, or hungry, or destitute, or in danger, or threatened with death?…No, despite all these things, overwhelming victory is ours through Christ, who loved us. (Romans 8:35, 37 NLT)

Notice that phrase "all these things." This passage isn't saying we won't face some of these struggles, but that in them we're "more than conquerors."

If you're seeking to obey the Lord, expect opposition. Expect obstacles. Expect difficulties. But also expect God to see you through.

> ## THE LORD'S INVITATION TO HIS PEOPLE
>
> Hope in God and wait expectantly for Him.
> PSALM 42:11 AMP

WITH GOD IN PRAYER

Ask Him what He wants you to learn in whatever difficulties you are now facing. And give Him praise for how He will lead you triumphantly through these obstacles.

MOVE BEYOND DESPAIR

What specific action steps has God shown you to take in light of your current circumstances or difficulties? Do today what you know He wants you to do, and trust Him for the results.

Your own reflections...personal application... personal prayer points...

People Reaching People

It's worth noting that in the New Testament we see no one coming to faith apart from the agency of another human being. Have you ever stopped and thought about that?

We can find example after example. Take the Ethiopian eunuch in Acts 8:26–39. There are many ways God could have reached this man from a distant country. He could have sent an angel to meet him; instead, the Lord sent an angel to Philip, who sent Philip to the Ethiopian. Philip obeyed. He went and proclaimed the gospel to that man, and the Ethiopian believed.

> So we are **Christ's** ambassadors; God is making his **appeal** through us.
> 2 CORINTHIANS 5:20 NLT

Then there was the Philippian jailer in Acts 16:27–34. God could have reached him without human help. Instead, He allowed Paul and Silas to be incarcerated in his jail. From these two prisoners, the jailer heard the gospel, and he and his family came to faith.

I think also of Cornelius in Acts 10, a centurion searching for God. An angel told him he needed to meet someone named Simon Peter, and the angel explained where to find him. Interesting. The angel could have given him the gospel. Instead God chose to use Simon Peter.

> So faith comes from hearing, that is,
> hearing the **Good News** about Christ.
>
> ROMANS 10:17 NLT

And what about Saul (later the apostle Paul) in Acts 9? While it's true he was converted through an encounter with Christ Himself on the Damascus Road, God sent Ananias to confirm this with Saul and to pray for him to receive the power of the Holy Spirit.

So you see, God uses people. And He wants to use you.

THE LORD'S INVITATION TO HIS PEOPLE

Live wisely among those who are not believers,
and make the most of every opportunity.

COLOSSIANS 4:5 NLT

WITH GOD IN PRAYER

Ask Him to show you clearly the people whose lives He wants you to invest in with your time and energy.

MOVE BEYOND FEELING USELESS

God wants to use you in the lives of unbelievers around you. Who are they? What can you do for them today? When can you share the gospel with them?

Your own reflections...personal application... personal prayer points...

When We Doubt

Oswald Chambers said, "Doubt is not always a sign that a man is wrong. It may be a sign that he is thinking." There's a difference between doubt and unbelief. Doubt is a matter of the mind. Unbelief is a matter of the heart. Doubt is when we cannot understand what God is doing or why He's doing it. Unbelief is when we refuse to believe God's Word and to do what He tells us to do. We must not confuse the two.

Remember the discouraged disciples on the Emmaus road in Luke 24? In their minds, Jesus had failed in His mission and had been crucified. Jesus joined them on that road and began to speak with them. Afterward they said, "Didn't our hearts burn within us as he talked with us on the road and explained the Scriptures to us?" (Luke 24:32 NLT). God dealt with their doubt through His Word.

> O you of little **faith**, why did you doubt?
> JESUS, IN MATTHEW 14:31

And God will deal with your doubt through His Word. When you're facing doubt, that's not the time to close the Bible. It's the time to open it and let God speak to you.

Maybe you've been doubting God's ways in your life. Maybe you've been asking *Why?* a lot lately. Maybe His timing doesn't seem to make any sense. Be confident that it will all be resolved in that final day when we stand before God. As Paul says,

Now we see things imperfectly as in a cloudy mirror, but then we will see everything with perfect clarity. All that I know now is partial and incomplete, but then I will know everything completely, just as God now knows me completely. (1 Corinthians 13:12 NLT)

God doesn't ask us to understand everything. He asks us to trust Him and follow Him.

THE LORD'S INVITATION TO HIS PEOPLE

If any of you lacks wisdom, let him ask of God,
who gives to all liberally and without reproach,
and it will be given to him.
But let him ask in faith, with no doubting,
for he who doubts is like a wave of the sea
driven and tossed by the wind.

JAMES 1:5–6

WITH GOD IN PRAYER

Be honest with Him about any doubts you're now experiencing.

MOVE BEYOND DOUBT

To help you overcome doubt, what are the truths about God and His character that you most need to remember?

Your own reflections...personal application... personal prayer points...

A Matter
of the Heart

It's fascinating to note how Jesus dealt with different people. He never dealt with any two individuals in precisely the same way. That's because He looked beyond the outward veneers and saw their hearts.

When a person was really seeking God and a miracle was in order, Jesus did one. There are numerous miracles He did for hurting, searching people like blind Bartimaeus, or the centurion whose servant was deathly ill, or the sick woman who spent everything on doctors and needed a miracle, or the ten lepers who came to Him looking for His cleansing touch.

> You will seek Me and **find** Me, when you
> **search** for Me with all your heart.
> JEREMIAH 29:13

But when people came to Jesus with the wrong motives, it was a different story. In fact, on some occasions, He didn't even reveal Himself to them, as in this instance:

Now when He was in Jerusalem at the Passover, during the feast, many believed in His name when they saw the signs which He did. But Jesus did not commit Himself to them, because He knew all men, and had no need that anyone should testify of man, for He knew what was in man. (John 2:23–25)

Here were these people who believed after they saw Jesus's miracles, but He wouldn't "commit" Himself to them. That really seems strange, doesn't it? But let's consider what the word *commit* means: to entrust someone with something. Jesus wouldn't entrust these people with His truth. If they were true seekers, Jesus would have revealed Himself to them.

These people weren't seeking with their whole hearts. They were merely excited about the miracles Jesus had done. Therefore, Jesus wouldn't commit Himself to them.

THE LORD'S INVITATION TO HIS PEOPLE

Seek the LORD while He may be found,
call upon Him while He is near.

ISAIAH 55:6

WITH GOD IN PRAYER

Thank Him for being so open and responsive to all who genuinely seek Him.

MOVE BEYOND FEELING DISTANT FROM GOD

What can you do today to more wholeheartedly seek the Lord?

Your own reflections...personal application... personal prayer points...

When God Seems to Disappoint

Have you ever had something happen in your life that caused you to say, *Where is God?* Someone no less than the greatest prophet who ever lived, John the Baptist, faced this same struggle.

John had put everything on the line for Jesus Christ. He had baptized Jesus in the Jordan River. He pointed his own disciples to Jesus, whom he believed was the Messiah. John had clearly pledged his complete loyalty to Jesus.

Then a strange series of events occurred that resulted in John's being arrested. One moment he was out preaching to the multitudes and baptizing people; the next moment he was in prison. And while there, the great John the Baptist began to entertain some doubt about Jesus. So he sent his disciples to Him with basically this question: "Are you really the One we've been waiting for? Or should we wait for somebody else?"

> John the Baptist, who was in prison, heard about all the things the **Messiah** was doing. So he sent his disciples to ask **Jesus**, "Are you the Messiah we've been expecting, or should we keep looking for **someone** else?"
>
> MATTHEW 11:2-3 NLT

Jesus's disciples commonly believed (as John did) that Jesus would establish His kingdom then and there. But they failed to recognize that before

Christ would establish His kingdom, He would first suffer and die for the sins of humanity. John misunderstood the prophecies of Scripture and therefore thought Jesus wasn't doing what He was supposed to do.

Sometimes we, too, misunderstand God and His Word when He doesn't do what we think He should do, or when He doesn't work as quickly as we would like Him to. But even when we cannot understand God's ways, His methods, or His timing, He still asks us to trust Him. And He is trustworthy.

THE LORD'S INVITATION TO HIS PEOPLE

Commit everything you do to the LORD.
Trust him, and he will help you.
PSALM 37:5 NLT

WITH GOD IN PRAYER

If there's anything about His ways of dealing with you that you don't understand, confess and acknowledge that He knows best and that all His ways are good and right.

MOVE BEYOND DISAPPOINTMENT WITH GOD

Commit to Him every part of your life, including especially those areas where God's timing or methods are hard for you to accept.

Your own reflections...personal application... personal prayer points...

The Message Proclaimed

The good news of Jesus Christ is meant to be proclaimed—to be preached. As Paul said of those who need salvation, "How shall they believe in Him of whom they have not heard? And how shall they hear without a preacher?" (Romans 10:14). That last question could also be translated (from the original Greek), "How shall they hear without someone preaching?" The J. B. Phillips translation puts it this way: "How can they hear unless someone proclaims him?" The emphasis is on preaching, not on a preacher.

We may think the work of evangelism is only for those who are called to be evangelists. Granted, there are people in the church whom God has raised up to be evangelists, but certainly evangelism isn't limited to those who preach to hundreds or thousands at a time. I've seen many individual believers who obviously have the gift of personal evangelism.

While it's true some are called to be evangelists, it's also true that every Christian is called to share the gospel with others.

> How **beautiful** are the feet of
> those who preach the gospel of peace,
> who bring glad tidings of **good** things!
> ROMANS 10:15

Many times, however, we avoid sharing our faith, deciding instead that it's sufficient to just live out our faith as good witnesses, and we leave the preaching to others. But think about the power of the spoken message of the gospel:

For since, in the wisdom of God, the world through wisdom did not know God, it pleased God through the foolishness of the message preached to save those who believe. (1 Corinthians 1:21)

The gospel is powerful enough to save those who believe, even though the message can seem foolish. This doesn't mean we need to scream and yell and wave a Bible to get our point across. It does mean we're to recognize that the primary way God has chosen to reach the lost is through the proclamation— by people—of the gospel. God has chosen the agency of His proclaimed Word to bring sinners to salvation.

THE LORD'S INVITATION TO HIS PEOPLE

Do not be afraid, but speak,
and do not keep silent; for I am with you.
ACTS 18:9–10

WITH GOD IN PRAYER

Give thanks to God for the privilege of being called to share the gospel with those who are lost.

MOVE BEYOND RELUCTANCE TO SHARE THE GOSPEL

Who are the lost people in your world who need to hear and believe the gospel? What can you do at once to present this good news to them?

Your own reflections...personal application... personal prayer points...

From His Perspective

I heard the story of an elderly minister who liked to visit people in hospitals. He often took along a little embroidered bookmark that he carried in his Bible. On the back, it looked like only a tangle of threads with no apparent pattern.

He would hand this bookmark, with its tangled back facing up, to those who were hurting or upset and say, "Look at this and tell me what it says."

As they looked at all the tangled threads, they would typically answer, "I have no idea. It doesn't seem to say anything."

"Turn it over," he would say. As they flipped over the bookmark, they saw the embroidered words, *God is love.* The minister would explain, "Many times as we look at what God is doing, we just see tangled threads with no rhyme or reason. But from God's perspective, He's dealing with us in love, and He knows what He's doing."

The next time you think it's all over for you, just remember how things finally turned out for Joseph with his dreams. Or how events finally turned out for Daniel after he was thrown in the den of lions and things looked hopeless. It looked hopeless as well for Shadrach, Meshach, and Abed-Nego when they were thrown into the fiery furnace. Things looked pretty grim for the apostle Peter when he was in prison. And things looked bleak for Martha and Mary when their brother died. But remember what happened to them all.

With God all things are possible.
JESUS, IN MATTHEW 19:26

You see, sometimes things can look bad, but suddenly God will step in and turn events around. Then you'll look back and say, "Now I understand what God was doing."

The Lord's Invitation to His People

Trust in Him at all times, you people; pour out your heart before Him; God is a refuge for us.
PSALM 62:8

With God in Prayer

Let Him know where you want Him to be at work in your life—to step in and turn things around.

Move Beyond Your Limited Perspective

Take time in the Scriptures to look closer at the stories of one or more of the Bible personalities mentioned above.

Your own reflections...personal application... personal prayer points...

Proclaiming Christ

These days, people are standing up and being counted for many causes. In fact, I'm amazed at the perverse, even horrendous things people will speak up for or even be willing to die for.

And yet Christians—who possess the life-changing message of the gospel—often keep quiet in shame or embarrassment about what the gospel has to say.

> We do not **preach** ourselves, but Christ Jesus the Lord, and ourselves your **bondservants** for Jesus' sake.
>
> 2 Corinthians 4:5

It's time for us to stand up and be counted as well. Jesus said,

Whoever is ashamed of Me and My words in this adulterous and sinful generation, of him the Son of Man also will be ashamed when He comes in the glory of His Father with the holy angels. (Mark 8:38)

In the first century, the thought of Jesus dying on the cross was scandalous to the Jews. The same thought was merely nonsense to the Greeks, who prided themselves on their cultural and intellectual attainments.

But the gospel is *power*—as the apostle Paul reminds us:

We preach Christ crucified, to the Jews a stumbling block and to the Greeks foolishness, but to those who are called, both Jews and Greeks, Christ the power of God and the wisdom of God. (1 Corinthians 1:23–24)

THE LORD'S INVITATION TO HIS PEOPLE

Thus it is written...that repentance
and remission of sins should be preached
in His name to all nations.
LUKE 24:46–47

WITH GOD IN PRAYER

Pray by name for unbelievers who have been brought into your life by God.

MOVE BEYOND KEEPING QUIET

Let God show you the power of the gospel. Share the good news with someone today.

Your own reflections...personal application... personal prayer points...

Beyond Excuses

The Pharisees who opposed Jesus were not simply doubting the work of God; their hearts were filled with unbelief. These religious leaders didn't reject Jesus and His messiahship for lack of evidence, because He had fulfilled many Old Testament prophesies. They didn't reject Him because of a lifestyle inconsistent with His preaching, because Jesus was absolutely perfect in His behavior. Even Pilate, as he was preparing to condemn Jesus to death, said this: "I find no fault in Him" (John 19:4). Judas Iscariot, His betrayer, said this: "I have betrayed innocent blood" (Matthew 27:4 NIV).

The Pharisees hardened their hearts against Jesus because He interfered with the way they'd chosen to live. He was a threat to their lifestyle and their religious system. In spite of all their rhetoric and claims of interest in spiritual things, they weren't really searching for the truth. Nor were they searching for the Messiah. Otherwise, they would have embraced Jesus.

> And **this** is the condemnation, that
> the light has come into the **world**,
> and men **loved** darkness rather than
> light, because their **deeds** were evil.
> JOHN 3:19

Their rejection of Him was for the same ultimate reason that people reject Him today. People don't reject Jesus Christ because they've examined the evidence and concluded He doesn't meet the qualifications for the Messiah. Most non-Christian people I talk to say they've never read the Bible. They haven't even read the gospel of John. They've never carefully examined the claims of Christ.

Nor do people reject Jesus because of the hypocrisy of some inconsistent Christians. People reject Jesus Christ because He's a threat to their lifestyle. They don't want to change. They want things left as they are; they hate the light that will expose their deeds.

THE LORD'S INVITATION TO HIS PEOPLE

Let your speech always be with grace,
seasoned with salt, that you may know
how you ought to answer each one.
COLOSSIANS 4:6

WITH GOD IN PRAYER

Ask Him to cause His Holy Spirit to break down the hatred for God's light that is evident in the lives of unbelievers you know.

MOVE BEYOND EXCUSES

Talk with an unbeliever today about his or her resistance to God's light and to change.

Your own reflections...personal application... personal prayer points...

Striking at the Root

Over the years, I've received many invitations to get involved in certain causes or to join a boycott or a march. I admire people who get out there and want to stand up for what's right, and I think we as Christians need to make our presence known in this culture and society.

But I personally have chosen to strike at the root of our society's problem—which is sin. I've chosen to seek to help our culture and our world by preaching the gospel. Why? Because although a change in one's lifestyle doesn't bring about salvation, true salvation will always bring about a change in one's lifestyle.

When Paul went to Rome, there were many social ills there he could have addressed. Rome was a city filled with slaves, yet Paul wouldn't center his preaching on slavery. Rome was a city of rampant immorality, but Paul's message didn't center on moral reform. Rome was a city of financial corruption, but Paul wouldn't center his preaching on the ethical problems of the marketplace. Instead, he chose to strike at the root of the problem. His message was simple. He gave them the gospel.

> I **decided** that while I was with you
> I would forget everything except **Jesus**
> Christ, the **one** who was crucified.
> 1 CORINTHIANS 2:2 NLT

I can work to bring reform and morality to my culture and society. I can work to help get laws passed to slow down the spread of sin and corruption.

But if I can lead others to Christ, then their morals and their lifestyles will ultimately change. Not only will they have the hope of heaven, but they'll also be different people in our society and culture.

THE LORD'S INVITATION TO HIS PEOPLE

Go into all the world and
preach the gospel to every creature.
MARK 16:15

WITH GOD IN PRAYER

Ask God to help you clearly communicate the gospel in your conversations with others.

MOVE BEYOND ADDRESSING ONLY SYMPTOMS

Talk with a non-Christian today about how the gospel of Jesus Christ is the only pathway of lasting change for the good in people's morals and behavior.

Your own reflections...personal application... personal prayer points...

Preaching the Cross

We may look with some envy on first-century believers who seemed to witness miracles as part of their daily lives. Certainly, there were dramatic miracles that took place during their time. In Acts we read of such great things happening as the lame beggar at the Beautiful Gate receiving the ability to walk, and Peter being released from prison by an angel, and the woman Dorcas being raised from the dead. We can look back on that time with fondness and say, "Those were the good ol' days."

As we read the book of Acts, it almost appears as though miracles happened every twelve minutes. But the truth is that Acts is a record of what God did over a thirty-year period. In other words, realistically, we should recognize that it's a record of miracles taking place over a long period of time.

Some Christians may think that if they could perform a sign or miracle for the unbelievers they know, then those people would believe. But the sign they need to know about is what Jesus accomplished on the cross. It's the preaching of the cross that will make the difference. "For the message of the cross…is the power of God" (1 Corinthians 1:18).

> Jews request a sign, and Greeks seek after wisdom; but we preach Christ **crucified**, to the Jews a stumbling block and to the Greeks foolishness, but to those who are called, **both** Jews and Greeks, Christ the power of God and the **wisdom** of God.
>
> 1 CORINTHIANS 1:22-24

"We preach Christ crucified," Paul said. That's also our message. That's what we have to say. So we can have the same commitment Paul had: "I determined not to know anything among you except Jesus Christ and Him crucified" (1 Corinthians 2:2).

Though I believe in miracles and hope to see more in my lifetime, one thing will never change—the simple message we must proclaim.

THE LORD'S INVITATION TO HIS PEOPLE

Proclaim the good news of
His salvation from day to day.
PSALM 96:2

WITH GOD IN PRAYER

Offer Him thanksgiving for the cross of Jesus Christ, and how for you and every human being it solves our greatest problem—the problem of sin.

MOVE BEYOND A LACK
OF APPRECIATION FOR THE CROSS

Who do you need to share with today the good news of the Cross of Christ Jesus?

Your own reflections...personal application... personal prayer points...

Walking
with Wisdom

Today we have people who seek a spiritual experience for the sake of experience, wanting to have what they think is "a touch from God." We have self-proclaimed prophets who give their messages and proclaim their visions but are rarely held accountable for the outcome.

We must be careful. On the one hand, we don't want to limit God through unbelief, because we want Him to do His miracles in our lives. On the other hand, we simply cannot believe everyone and everything.

I believe in miracles. I believe in the supernatural. I believe God can heal. But we cannot seek experience at any cost. Experience must always be subservient to truth. It must always be ordered under what's right. We cannot say something is true and right simply because we've experienced it. Rather, we should know something is true and right because it's found in Scripture, and we allow Scripture to verify our experience.

> Many will say to Me in that day,
> "Lord, Lord, have we not **prophesied** in
> Your name, cast out demons in Your name,
> and done many **wonders** in Your name?"
> And then I will declare to them,
> "I never knew you; depart from Me,
> you who practice **lawlessness**!"
> JESUS, IN MATTHEW 7:22-23

In the book of Acts, we never read about a miracle announced ahead of time. When God used Peter to heal the lame beggar at the Beautiful Gate (see Acts 3), we don't read that it was first advertised: "Be at the Beautiful Gate today! Miracles! Signs! Wonders! Don't miss it!" The apostles never announced miracles in advance because their focus wasn't on miracles. Their focus was on proclaiming the Word of God. They left miracles up to the Holy Spirit.

We must be especially careful in these last days, because not all signs and miracles come from God. Remember, Satan is a great imitator.

THE LORD'S INVITATION TO HIS PEOPLE

Test all things; hold fast what is good.
1 THESSALONIANS 5:21

WITH GOD IN PRAYER

Ask Him to give you the discernment you need to understand how He works.

MOVE BEYOND OVERRATING EXPERIENCE

Identify the kinds of situations in which you're most likely to overrate your own (or someone else's) experience without using Scripture to verify the validity of it. What can you do to change?

Your own reflections...personal application... personal prayer points...

Unlikely Conversions

An attorney was trying to deliver an important paper to a man, but the man thought it was some type of subpoena, so he went out of his way to dodge the attorney.

Fourteen years passed, and the man found himself in the hospital, dying of cancer. Through a strange series of events, the attorney was admitted to the hospital for an illness and was assigned to the same room as the dying man.

The man turned to the attorney and said, "Well, you never got me. I've escaped you all this time, and now it doesn't matter. You can even serve your subpoena. I don't care."

The lawyer replied, "Subpoena? I was trying to give you a document that proved you'd inherited forty-five million dollars!"

Many people go out of their way to avoid Christians and the opportunity to have a relationship with Jesus Christ. All the while, their hearts grow harder, and they risk becoming callous to the point of no return. We don't know when that point will come in their lives. Maybe you even know someone who seems as though he's reached it.

> Today, if you will hear His **voice**,
> do not harden your hearts.
> HEBREWS 4:7

We can take heart when we look at the conversion of Saul of Tarsus. The change in him was so radical and unexpected that when it became known, first-century Christians thought Saul was attempting to infiltrate their ranks and persecute the believers even more. They didn't believe God could save someone as wicked and hostile toward the Christians as Saul had been. But as we know, Saul became Paul the apostle.

If you know someone who seems so far gone and permanently hardened toward the gospel, keep praying. You never know; that person just might be the next Paul.

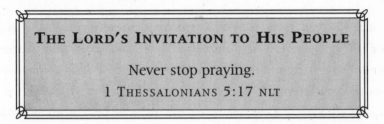

THE LORD'S INVITATION TO HIS PEOPLE

Never stop praying.

1 THESSALONIANS 5:17 NLT

WITH GOD IN PRAYER

Think of those you know who seem hardened to the gospel, and ask God to change their hearts.

MOVE BEYOND DOUBTS THAT GOD CAN SAVE THE HARDHEARTED

Pray today for those you know personally who seem hardest to reach with the gospel.

Your own reflections...personal application... personal prayer points...

Undefeated

Through the years, many have set themselves against the church and tried to destroy it. In the reign of the Roman emperor Diocletian, Christians were martyred, and Scriptures and churches were destroyed. To commemorate these accomplishments, he set up a stone pillar of victory with this inscription: *Extinco nomine Christianorum* ("the name of the Christian has been extinguished"). I wonder how Diocletian would feel if he could see that monument today. His "accomplishments" obviously didn't last.

There have been those who have tried to stop the work of God. One Roman leader made a coffin to symbolize his intention, in his words, to "bury the Galilean" by killing His followers. But he soon learned he couldn't put Jesus in that coffin. Finally, he ended up believing in the One he tried to destroy.

Closer to our own time, Communist governments have tried to stamp out the church. But nothing and no one has ever been able to stop the church—because Jesus established it, and He said:

> I will **build** my church, and the gates
> of hell shall not **prevail** against it.
> JESUS, IN MATTHEW 16:18 ESV

"The gates of hell" refers to the forces of the devil, and when Jesus says the gates of hell shall not prevail against the church, He isn't saying these forces won't try to attack us. When we attempt to get the gospel out, the devil will oppose us with everything he has. But as we move forward as soldiers in the Lord's army, the devil's opposition will not prevail.

We may lose a battle here and there. But clearly, the devil will lose the war in the end—and Jesus and His church will win.

The Lord's Invitation to His People

Thanks be to God, who gives us the
victory through our Lord Jesus Christ.
Therefore, my beloved brethren, be steadfast,
immovable, always abounding in the work
of the Lord, knowing that your labor
is not in vain in the Lord.

1 Corinthians 15:57–58

With God in Prayer

Give Him thanks that you are on His winning side—and that ultimately all the devil's opposition against Him will fail.

Move Beyond the Devil's Opposition

What can help you keep from getting discouraged when you encounter attacks from the devil?

Your own reflections...personal application... personal prayer points...

His Will, Not Mine

There are some people who teach that we should never pray, *Not my will, but Yours be done,* because it supposedly voids what you've just prayed for. What nonsense! If Jesus prayed this, certainly we should follow His example. He gave us the same pattern in the Lord's Prayer when He said, "May your Kingdom come soon. May your will be done on earth, as it is in heaven" (Matthew 6:10 NLT). I never need to be afraid to say, *Lord, Your will be done.*

Then there are those who say we should pray for something only once; otherwise, we're demonstrating a lack of faith. Yet Jesus taught His disciples, "Keep on asking, and you will receive what you ask for. Keep on seeking, and you will find. Keep on knocking, and the door will be opened to you" (Luke 11:9 NLT). We give up far too easily sometimes.

> He **went** on a little farther and bowed
> with his face to the ground, **praying**,
> "My Father! If it is possible, let this cup
> of **suffering** be taken away from me. Yet
> I want your **will** to be done, not mine."
> JESUS, IN MATTHEW 26:39 NLT

We won't always know the will of God in every situation. At other times, we do know the will of God, but we don't like it. There are also times when we know the will of God, but we don't understand it.

I like what D. L. Moody said: "Spread out your petition before God, and then say, 'Thy will, not mine, be done.'" Moody concluded, "The sweetest lesson I have learned in God's school is to let the Lord choose for me."

Have you found that to be true in your own life?

We must never be afraid to trust an unknown future to a known God.

THE LORD'S INVITATION TO HIS PEOPLE

As slaves of Christ,
do the will of God with all your heart.

EPHESIANS 6:6 NLT

WITH GOD IN PRAYER

Confess honestly your level of trust in God as it relates to your future.

MOVE BEYOND YOUR FEAR OF FUTURE UNKNOWNS

Recognize the paths and directions that God has clearly led you to. What does this show you about your future?

Your own reflections...personal application... personal prayer points...

The Reason for Rejection

Why do people reject Jesus Christ without ever taking time to consider His claims? Why do people reject the revelation of Scripture when in most cases they've never taken time to read it carefully for themselves? Why do people refuse to give at least a fair hearing to the message of the gospel?

We find the answer in Scripture. Jesus said,

> God's light came into the world, but people loved the darkness more than the light, for their actions were evil. (John 3:19 NLT)

Someone may say, "The reason I'm not a Christian is because I disagree with this," or, "I have problems with that." But according to Jesus, the real reason is that their deeds are evil. They don't want to come into the light, where their deeds will be exposed. Anything else is merely an excuse people try to hide behind.

> The leading **priests** and the entire high council were trying to find witnesses who would lie about **Jesus**, so they could put him to death.
> MATTHEW 26:59 NLT

I'm not saying people don't have legitimate questions to ask. I'm not saying people don't grapple with some of these truths. What I'm saying is that when people are true seekers of God—when they honestly recognize their sinfulness and their need for salvation—they will believe when they're presented with the answers to their questions about Christ and the gospel.

> ## THE LORD'S INVITATION TO HIS PEOPLE
>
> You were once darkness, but now you
> are light in the Lord. Walk as children of light.
> EPHESIANS 5:8

WITH GOD IN PRAYER

Acknowledge before God how your own sin has blinded you—now or in the past—to the truth about Him.

MOVE BEYOND EXCUSES

Confess and repent of any sins that continue to block or distort your view of the Lord and the gospel.

Your own reflections...personal application... personal prayer points...

Like Sheep

On more than one occasion, the Bible compares Christians to sheep. I don't know if I'm really happy about that, because sheep are not the most intelligent animals on earth.

It would have been nice if God had compared us to dolphins. Now there's an intelligent animal. I once had the opportunity to talk to a man who trained dolphins. I asked him, "Are dolphins really as intelligent as they seem?" He said, "In some ways, yes, and in some ways, no. They're very intelligent in many ways, because a dolphin can see a symbol and understand what it means." That's amazing to me.

But Jesus didn't compare us to dolphins. He compared us to sheep. And sheep are some of the stupidest animals around. They're easily spooked. They're vulnerable. They have no defense mechanisms to speak of. They can't run very fast. They're in constant need of care and attention. They have a horrible tendency to follow one another, even to their own deaths. It has been documented that if one sheep walks off a cliff, the others will follow.

> Once you were like **sheep** who wandered away. But now you have turned to your **Shepherd**, the Guardian of your souls.
> 1 PETER 2:25 NLT

The Bible says, "All of us, like sheep, have strayed away. We have left God's paths to follow our own" (Isaiah 53:6 NLT). Think about how many people have bought into the same lies, generation after generation. They fall into the same junk, the same addictions, and the same traps again and again.

We are like sheep. That's a fact. The question is, are you going to be a smart sheep or a dumb one? Smart sheep stay close to the Shepherd, and that's where we all need to be.

THE LORD'S INVITATION TO HIS PEOPLE

If anyone serves Me, let him follow Me;
and where I am, there My servant will be also.
JESUS, IN JOHN 12:26

WITH GOD IN PRAYER

Confess to Him the ways you know you have strayed like a sheep.

MOVE BEYOND STUPIDITY

What do you need to do today to stay closer to your Shepherd all day long?

Your own reflections...personal application... personal prayer points...

Crucified with Christ

When Jesus referred to taking up the cross, I'm sure the meaning wasn't lost on the disciples. The cross, as the people knew in that time and culture, was a hated and despised symbol of an extremely cruel death. The Romans crucified many people on the roads leading into their cities as a warning to any man or woman who would dare defy the powers of Rome. The cross was meant to humiliate. It was meant to torture. Ultimately, it was meant to kill.

Today, the cross is shrouded in religiosity. It has become a symbol of many things, from a religious icon to an ornate piece of jewelry. It isn't necessarily a bad thing to wear a cross, but I think we've lost the meaning of it. Imagine wearing a little replica of an electric chair around your neck, studded in diamonds, or maybe a little hangman's noose. Wearing jewelry like that would be rather morbid, because those are symbols of death and pain. But that's what the cross symbolized. So when Jesus told the disciples that if anyone wanted to follow him, he must take up his cross, they would readily understand what He was speaking of.

> Whoever does not bear his **cross** and come after Me cannot be My disciple.
> JESUS, IN LUKE 14:27

The cross speaks of dying to self, of putting God's will before our own. If this sounds like a horrible, negative lifestyle, consider Paul's words: "I have been crucified with Christ; it is no longer I who live, but Christ lives in me" (Galatians 2:20). It's through death that we find life. May God help us to see that His trade-in deal is the best there is.

> ### THE LORD'S INVITATION TO HIS PEOPLE
>
> If anyone desires to come after Me,
> let him deny himself, and take up his cross,
> and follow Me.
> JESUS, IN MATTHEW 16:24

WITH GOD IN PRAYER

Honestly express your gratefulness for Christ's death on the cross. Thank Him for what He accomplished there specifically for you.

MOVE BEYOND SELF-CENTEREDNESS

Christ's death makes true life possible for you...as you die to self and allow Him to live His life through you. What selfish pursuits or attitudes do you need to let go of today to let His life take control?

Your own reflections...personal application... personal prayer points...

Walking with Jesus

It's interesting to note those to whom Jesus chose to appear after His resurrection. If it had been me, the first person I would have appeared to would have been Pilate: "Yo, Pilate! Remember me? Can't keep a good man down, can you?" Or, I would have appeared to Caiaphas, the high priest who, for the most part, orchestrated the crucifixion of Jesus.

But we don't read about Him appearing to Pilate or Caiaphas. We do read in Luke 24:13–35 about His appearance to two disciples on the road to Emmaus and how He joined them on their journey. We know the name of one of these two men (Cleopas); other than that, we know nothing about them, and they aren't mentioned again in the Bible.

Luke tells us that when Jesus came alongside them on the road, "their eyes were restrained, so that they did not know Him" (24:16). After all, the last sight they'd had of Him was His beaten and bloodied body. Surely they wanted to get that image out of their minds. Mark says of this incident that Jesus appeared to them "in another form" (16:12). In other words, He was incognito.

There they were, walking along, and Jesus was walking with them. It's a reminder to us that at all times, even when we don't realize it, He's walking with us.

> He **appeared** in another form
> to two of them as they walked
> and **went** into the country.
> MARK 16:12

The Lord makes this promise to His people: "When you pass through the waters, I will be with you; and through the rivers, they shall not overflow you. When you walk through the fire, you shall not be burned, nor shall the flame scorch you" (Isaiah 43:2).

Maybe you feel close to God only when you're in church. But wherever you go, you can know Jesus is with you there too. When you're going through hard times, even when you cannot feel His presence, Jesus is there.

THE LORD'S INVITATION TO HIS PEOPLE

Be strong and of good courage;
do not be afraid, nor be dismayed, for the
LORD your God is with you wherever you go.

JOSHUA 1:9

WITH GOD IN PRAYER

Thank the Lord for His unfailing presence with you. Talk with Him about your desire to sense His presence more deeply.

MOVE BEYOND FEELING ALONE

What do you need to remind yourself of when you feel distant from God?

Your own reflections...personal application... personal prayer points...

True Disciples

The Christian life is more than just saying a prayer or walking down an aisle and getting "fire insurance." The Christian life is meant to be dynamic. It's meant to be exciting. It's meant to have a radical effect upon the way you live and upon your outlook on life. Jesus Christ not only wants to be your Savior, He wants to be your Lord. He wants to be not only your friend, but also your God.

But I'm afraid many Christians today are living a substandard Christian experience. That term is really an oxymoron in many ways, because if it's truly a Christian experience, it shouldn't be substandard. In a sense, that isn't even a technically correct term. You really can't be a substandard Christian.

> The disciples were **filled** with
> **joy** and with the Holy Spirit.
> ACTS 13:52

Yet there are many who are failing to receive all God has for them.

In Acts 17:6 the first-century Christians are described as people "who have turned the world upside down." How did a handful of ordinary people turn their world (as they knew it) upside down? They did it without television, radio, or the Internet, without megachurches, and without all the resources we think are so important today in reaching the goal of world evangelism.

How were they able to do it? I think you could sum it up in one word: disciple. They were disciples of Jesus Christ—not fair-weather followers, but true disciples. They weren't living an anemic, watered-down, ineffective version of the Christian life. They were living the Christian life as it was meant to be lived—as Christ Himself offered it and as the early disciples apprehended it.

If we want to impact our culture today, then we, too, must be disciples.

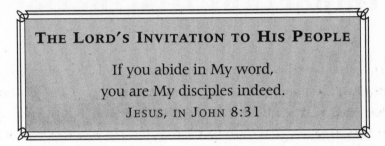

THE LORD'S INVITATION TO HIS PEOPLE

If you abide in My word,
you are My disciples indeed.
JESUS, IN JOHN 8:31

WITH GOD IN PRAYER

Thank Him for the picture of true discipleship that He gives us in the Scriptures. And talk with Him honestly about the ways you fall short of that picture.

MOVE BEYOND SUBSTANDARD CHRISTIANITY

Are you helping to turn your world upside down? To be a part of accomplishing this, what bold steps do you need to take today?

Your own reflections...personal application... personal prayer points...

Discipleship's Important Distinction

What does it mean to be a disciple? Certainly we need to know the answer to that question. After all, Jesus commanded us to go and make disciples of all nations.

But how can we make disciples if we aren't disciples ourselves? Are the qualifications of discipleship different from those of simply coming to faith?

I believe the answer is yes.

First, Jesus tells us that if we want to be His disciples, we must deny ourselves (see Luke 14:25–33). This is a foundational issue. We have a choice in life: We can either live for ourselves, or we can deny ourselves. We can either ignore the cross, or we can take it up and follow Him.

The great barrier to being a disciple of Jesus Christ is summed up in one word—self. Self-obsession isn't something unique to our generation, although the Bible does say that in the last days people will be lovers of themselves and lovers of pleasure more than lovers of God (see 2 Timothy 3:1–5). Certainly we're living in a time of great self-obsession in our culture. Yet we can trace its roots all the way back to the Garden of Eden. When Satan came to Eve, he essentially appealed to her selfish nature.

> Whoever does not **bear** his **cross** and come after Me cannot be My disciple.
> JESUS, IN LUKE 14:27

That's why Jesus said, "If anyone desires to come after Me, let him deny himself" (Matthew 16:24). Jesus didn't say, "Love yourself." He didn't say, "Have a positive self-image." He said you must deny yourself. That's what we need to do, because self is what gets in the way of true discipleship.

> ## THE LORD'S INVITATION TO HIS PEOPLE
>
> If anyone desires to come after Me,
> let him deny himself, and take up his cross,
> and follow Me.
>
> JESUS, IN MATTHEW 16:24

WITH GOD IN PRAYER

Ask him to show you how you need to get self out of the way.

MOVE BEYOND SELF-OBSESSION

In your life today, what does it really mean to be a disciple of Jesus Christ?

Your own reflections...personal application... personal prayer points...

Making Disciples

We find our "marching orders" from Jesus in Matthew 28:19–20, a passage we know as the Great Commission. There are two things we should especially remember about it.

First, these words are a command. That's why we call it the Great Commission and not the Great Suggestion. Jesus didn't say, "Look, if you're in the mood, if it works into your busy schedule, as a personal favor to Me, would you consider going into the world and making disciples?" No. This is a command.

Second, these words were not given exclusively to the original eleven disciples. Nor do they apply only to pastors, evangelists, and missionaries. They're for every follower of Jesus Christ. If we're His disciples, then we're commanded to go and make disciples of others. It doesn't necessarily mean we need to cross the sea. But certainly a good start would be crossing the street to talk to a neighbor.

What does it mean to make disciples? Jesus said, "Teach these new disciples to obey all the commands I have given you" (Matthew 28:20 NLT). Simply put, it means you demonstrate discipleship for them by the way you live. And of course, you also verbally communicate God's Word.

> We **tell** others about Christ, warning everyone and teaching every-one with all the wisdom God has **given** us. We want to present them to God, perfect in their **relationship** to Christ.
>
> COLOSSIANS 1:28 NLT

I want to challenge you today to become a disciple of Jesus Christ—not just a fair-weather follower or simply a churchgoing person. Would you be His disciple? If so, your life will never be the same—especially as you spend your life in helping others become His disciples.

THE LORD'S INVITATION TO HIS PEOPLE

All authority has been given to Me in heaven and on earth. Go therefore and make disciples of all the nations, baptizing them in the name of the Father and of the Son and of the Holy Spirit, teaching them to observe all things that I have commanded you; and lo, I am with you always, even to the end of the age.

JESUS, IN MATTHEW 28:18–20

WITH GOD IN PRAYER

Talk with Him about the people He wants you to help in becoming disciples of Jesus Christ. Pray for them by name.

MOVE BEYOND BEING LESS THAN A DISCIPLE

Today, in what specific ways can your life be a demonstration of what it means to be a disciple of Jesus Christ?

Your own reflections...personal application... personal prayer points...

On the Mountaintop

The transfiguration of Jesus was a significant event. It was the halfway point on a difficult journey. From here, Jesus went forward to the cross.

Jesus apparently believed the time was right for the disciples—specifically Peter, James, and John—to have a greater glimpse of His glory. Jesus singled these three out on a number of occasions. When He raised a ruler's daughter from the dead, He took Peter, James, and John inside the ruler's house with Him (see Mark 5:37; Luke 8:51). Later, He took these same three into the recesses of the Garden of Gethsemane to be with Him (see Matthew 26:37; Mark 14:33).

Perhaps they were the superspiritual disciples, the spiritual elite. Or maybe they just needed special attention. Whatever the reason, Jesus took these three with Him to the top of a high mountain, and He was transfigured before their eyes. His garments became as white as light. His face shone like the sun. Moses and Elijah were also there, which only added to the drama of this wonderful event.

> Jesus took Peter, John, and James up on a mountain to **pray**. And as he was **praying**, the appearance of his face was **transformed**, and his clothes became dazzling white.
> LUKE 9:28-29 NLT

Peter couldn't contain himself any longer. "As Moses and Elijah were starting to leave, Peter, not even knowing what he was saying, blurted out, 'Master, it's wonderful for us to be here! Let's make three shelters as memorials—one for you, one for Moses, and one for Elijah' " (Luke 9:33 NLT). Essentially Peter was saying, "Let's stay here. This is the right idea: You're glorified; You're shining. Let's just camp out here and keep it this way."

Believers today have a tendency to do this as well. As this world grows darker, we're inclined to withdraw into a Christian subculture instead of realizing there's a world in need around us. God wants us to reach the world with the gospel. But to do so, we need to come down from our mountaintops and live this Christian life in the real world.

THE LORD'S INVITATION TO HIS PEOPLE

Go and announce to them that the Kingdom of Heaven is near. Heal the sick, raise the dead, cure those with leprosy, and cast out demons. Give as freely as you have received!

JESUS, IN MATTHEW 10:7–8 NLT

WITH GOD IN PRAYER

Ask Him to show you any ways in which you're too withdrawn into the Christian subculture. Ask Him to give you more of His heart and compassion for the needy world around us.

MOVE BEYOND THE CHRISTIAN SUBCULTURE

Are there any ways in which you are too withdrawn into the Christian subculture? Which of those ways hinder your witness to the world? If so, identify these barriers and decide how to overcome them.

Your own reflections...personal application... personal prayer points...

Spiritual Slumber

Why did Peter say what he said during such a significant event as the Transfiguration? The Gospels give us two reasons. One, he didn't know what to say. And two, he was "heavy with sleep" (Luke 9:32).

This was a bad time to fall asleep. Imagine what else Peter might have seen had he been fully awake and watchful!

This, of course, wouldn't be the last time that Peter (along with James and John) would fall asleep while on watch. In the Garden of Gethsemane, Jesus told them to stay awake (see Matthew 26:38, Mark 14:34). Then He went a few feet away and began to pray. When He came back, they were all sleeping. They were missing out on a significant event in the life of the Lord.

> Couldn't you **watch** with me even one hour? Keep watch and pray, so that **you** will **not** give in to temptation. For the spirit is willing, but the body is weak.
> JESUS, IN MARK 14:37-38 NLT

I wonder how much we miss out on because of our spiritual slumber. How many times are we spiritually slumbering when God wants to speak to us through His Word? Because we're too preoccupied with other things, we don't have the discipline to pick up the Bible and open it. How many times are we spiritually slumbering instead of going to church and being fed from the Word of God? How many times are we spiritually slumbering when the Lord would want us to speak up for Him? We're asleep on the watch.

Like the disciples, we, too, can miss out on what God wants to do in and through us. We need to be awake. We need to be alert. We need to be paying attention.

THE LORD'S INVITATION TO HIS PEOPLE

We are not of the night nor of darkness.
Therefore let us not sleep, as others do,
but let us watch and be sober.

1 THESSALONIANS 5:5–6

WITH GOD IN PRAYER

If you've been in a spiritual slumber, humble yourself before the Lord and confess this to Him.

MOVE BEYOND SPIRITUAL SLUMBER

Today, what do you need to do to be awake, alert, and attentive to the Holy Spirit's leading?

Your own reflections...personal application... personal prayer points...

Letting God Choose

When my oldest son was a little boy, I would take him to Toys "R" Us. As we looked around, I would tell him to pick out something for himself. While he examined little Star Wars figures, I would look at the X-wing fighter with the remote control, thinking that's what I wanted to get for him (partly because I wanted to play with it too). When he showed a little Star Wars figure to me, I answered, "I was thinking of getting you something better than that." He always went along with my idea.

After a while, he started learning something: his dad liked to get presents for his kids. My son came to realize it was better to say, "I don't know what to get, Dad; you choose it for me." He came to realize that my choices were often better than what he chose for himself.

> All glory to God, who is **able**,
> through his mighty **power** at work
> within us, to accomplish infinitely
> **more** than we might ask or think.
> EPHESIANS 3:20 NLT

Have you ever said to the Lord, "Here's the way I think You ought to work. But not my will, but Yours be done"?

You might respond, "I'm not saying that to God. If I did, He'll make me do something I don't want to do." But to think in this way reflects a warped concept of God, a misconception that His will is always going to be something undesirable.

God may be saying no to something you've asked Him for because He wants to give you something far better than what you could ask or think. Don't be afraid to let your Father choose for you.

> ## THE LORD'S INVITATION TO HIS PEOPLE
>
> Don't act thoughtlessly, but understand
> what the Lord wants you to do.
> EPHESIANS 5:17 NLT

WITH GOD IN PRAYER

Thank Him that His choices for you are always better than yours.

MOVE BEYOND RESISTING GOD'S CHOICES

Right now, in what important areas of life is it most critical for you to be telling the Lord, "Not my will, but Yours"? Honestly evaluate whether you truly believe that His choices are better than yours in these areas.

Your own reflections...personal application... personal prayer points...

Tabloid Mentality

It seems as though we're living in a day of tabloid mentality. I've never seen a culture and society so obsessed with gossip, innuendos, and rumors. Just turn on the television, and you'll find all kinds of programs that probe into the personal lives of others.

This tabloid mentality has even entered the news media, where reporters hunt for juicy pieces of gossip. The tragedy is that whenever people are charged with crimes today, we try them in the media before they've ever had the opportunity to enter a court of law where evidence is presented and they face their accusers.

Sadly, this kind of thinking can even enter the church. When we hear something negative about someone else, immediately our ears perk up. But what does the Bible tell us? It says that love believes the best of every person; it doesn't say that love believes the worst.

This means that when someone says something about a Christian brother or sister, you should immediately have some disbelief in your heart. The reason is that you're to believe the best of that individual. We must be very careful, because many times we accept rumor as truth. Then, to make matters worse, we start repeating what we've heard without checking the facts.

> A troublemaker plants seeds of **strife**; gossip separates the best of **friends**.
>
> PROVERBS 16:28 NLT

In the Bible we learn that one of the things God hates is a person who sows discord among others (see Proverbs 6:16–19). This is the person who spreads rumors, who spreads innuendos, and who slanders others. God hates this.

Don't be someone who spreads rumors. Don't be someone who gossips. It's wrong. It's sinful. And it displeases God.

THE LORD'S INVITATION TO HIS PEOPLE

Do not spread slanderous gossip.
LEVITICUS 19:16 NLT

You must not pass along false rumors.
EXODUS 23:1 NLT

WITH GOD IN PRAYER

Praise Him for being a God of truth who hates falsehood as well as discord in His family. Confess any ways that you may have displeased Him in these areas.

MOVE BEYOND A TABLOID MENTALITY

Can you recall a conversation where you've indulged in gossip or false rumors? If so, go to whomever you were speaking with and apologize for this sin.

Your own reflections...personal application... personal prayer points...

Caring Enough to Confront

After observing some people's behavior, you would think their Bibles have a verse that says, "If someone is caught in a sin, go tell as many people as possible. Then try to drive that person away." But that isn't what Scripture tells us to do. In Matthew 18, Jesus gives us the steps we should take when it appears someone has fallen into sin (and I emphasize the word *appears*).

First, we must know all the facts. When you hear something about someone, instead of talking about it, determine to go to that person and say, "I heard this about you. Is it true?" Hopefully, you can get the issue resolved immediately.

> Dear brothers and sisters, if another **believer** is overcome by some sin, you who are godly should **gently** and humbly **help** that person back onto the right path. And be careful not to fall into the same **temptation** yourself.
>
> GALATIANS 6:1 NLT

But to fail to go to someone when you know a sin is being committed is to actually cause that individual, and the church as a whole, the greatest harm. Scripture says, "A little leaven leavens the whole lump" (Galatians 5:9). In most cases, believers rarely approach a sinning believer or an allegedly sinning believer. Instead of seeking to help a person who possibly may have never sinned at all, they end up slandering that individual. This is wrong. If you've ever had this happen to you, you know how painful it can be.

Remember, the devil wants to turn believers against one another. He'll attack us from the outside, but when that doesn't work, he often seeks to infiltrate our ranks and divide us.

THE LORD'S INVITATION TO HIS PEOPLE

If your brother sins against you, go and tell him his fault between you and him alone. If he hears you, you have gained your brother. But if he will not hear, take with you one or two more, that "by the mouth of two or three witnesses every word may be established." And if he refuses to hear them, tell it to the church. But if he refuses even to hear the church, let him be to you like a heathen and a tax collector.

JESUS, IN MATTHEW 18:15–17

WITH GOD IN PRAYER

Pray against the enemy's tactics for bringing disunity into your church and the body of Christ at this time. Ask the Lord to defeat these tactics.

MOVE BEYOND A LACK OF CARING

Is there a believer whom you need to confront about a sin? If so, decide when and where to confront this person, and ask God to strengthen you with wisdom, humility, and love as you speak.

Your own reflections...personal application... personal prayer points...

Why Forgive?

Talk about a person who'd been wronged! Joseph's brothers had done all kinds of horrible things to him. They betrayed him—their own flesh and blood—and sold him into slavery. But through an amazing course of events directed by the hand of God, Joseph became the second most powerful man in the world at that point in history.

The day came when his brothers were brought before him—the very ones who had betrayed him. With one word, they could have become headless brothers. It could have been Joseph's payback time. But look at what he said to his brothers:

> Don't be afraid of me. Am I God, that I can punish you? You intended to harm me, but God intended it all for good. He brought me to this position so I could save the lives of many people. (Genesis 50:19–20 NLT)

Did Joseph's brothers deserve to be forgiven? No. But if we resort to that kind of thinking, we must ask ourselves, "Do we deserve to be forgiven by God?" No. So we should forgive others as God has forgiven us.

Peter came to him and asked, "Lord, how often should I **forgive** someone who **sins** against me? Seven times?" "No, not seven times," Jesus replied, "but **seventy** times seven!"

MATTHEW 18:21-22 NLT

Forgive...and forget. There's no point in burying the hatchet if you're determined to mark the site. Let it go. Put it behind you. Move forward.

If you refuse to forgive people who have wronged you, you'll become a bitter person. The problem with bitterness is that it infects those around you (see Hebrews 12:14–15).

If someone has sinned against you, you must learn to forgive. I know it isn't an easy thing to do. But when you forgive someone, you release a prisoner—yourself.

THE LORD'S INVITATION TO HIS PEOPLE

Be kind to one another,
tenderhearted, forgiving one another,
even as God in Christ forgave you.
EPHESIANS 4:32

WITH GOD IN PRAYER

If you're battling with unforgiveness and bitterness toward someone who's sinned against you, confess this to God. Thank Him for the fullness of His forgiveness for you.

MOVE BEYOND THE FAILURE TO FORGIVE

How can you move forward positively in your relationships with those who need your forgiveness?

Your own reflections...personal application... personal prayer points...

Lord of All

It was George Bernard Shaw who said, "There are two sources of unhappiness in life. One is not getting what you want. The other is getting it."

This statement reminds me of the rich young ruler who came to Jesus seeking answers (see Matthew 19:16–22). Here was someone who, of all people, should have been content and fulfilled. He had great influence and affluence. Yet in spite of all this, something was missing in his life. He said to Jesus, "Good Teacher, what good thing shall I do that I may have eternal life?"

Jesus answered, "If you want to enter into life, keep the commandments." Jesus wasn't implying that it's possible for us to be saved by keeping the Ten Commandments. Rather, Jesus held the Ten Commandments up as a mirror to this man to show him his sin.

The ruler replied, "All these things I have kept from my youth. What do I still lack?"

I think Jesus probably smiled at this. He saw what this man was really all about. So He took it up a notch and said, "If you want to be perfect, go, sell what you have and give to the poor, and you will have treasure in heaven; and come, follow Me."

> Whoever of you does not **forsake**
> all that he has cannot be My disciple.
> JESUS, IN LUKE 14:33

Jesus knew the particular problem with this young ruler: possessions had possessed his soul. To someone else, Jesus might have pointed to something

completely different. The issues holding us back from Christ and from further
spiritual progress will vary from person to person.

We do well to come before Jesus and ask, *Lord, is there anything in my life
that's hindering my relationship with You?*

THE LORD'S INVITATION TO HIS PEOPLE

In your hearts set apart Christ as Lord.
1 PETER 3:15 NIV

WITH GOD IN PRAYER

Ask Him to show you any possessions, activities, or relationships that are hindering your relationship with Him. Acknowledge His ownership and authority
over these.

MOVE BEYOND OBSTACLES
IN YOUR RELATIONSHIP WITH JESUS

What possessions do you need to get rid of? What activities or relationships
do you need to step away from?

Your own reflections...personal application...
personal prayer points...

The Rewards of Right Choices

Jesus told a rich young ruler to sell his belongings and give the money to the poor; the young man decided he couldn't do what Jesus asked. As a result, "he went away sorrowful" (Matthew 19:22).

Peter had been listening in on the conversation. It revealed, beyond a shadow of a doubt, that possessions had possessed this young ruler's soul.

After seeing what this ruler couldn't give up, Peter spoke up: "See, we have left all and followed You. Therefore what shall we have?" (Matthew 19:27). In other words, "What's in it for us?"

Now, what did Peter actually leave? He left a few broken-down nets and a fishing boat. Granted, it wasn't a lot. But he left it behind.

Jesus answered him this way: "Assuredly, I say to you, there is no one who has left house or brothers or sisters or father or mother or wife or children or lands, for My sake and the gospel's, who shall not receive a hundredfold now in this time—houses and brothers and sisters and mothers and children and lands, with persecutions—and in the age to come, eternal life" (Mark 10:29–30).

Jesus was saying, "It will be made up to you, Peter."

He who does not **take** his cross and follow after Me is not worthy of Me. He who finds his life will **lose** it, and he who loses his life for My sake will **find** it.

JESUS, IN MATTHEW 10:38-39

This promise holds true today. Whatever you've given up for Jesus, it will be made up to you. Maybe you've lost a friendship here and there. Maybe you gave up a certain lifestyle. You've made changes in your life, as you should have, and those changes brought cost or loss. But God will make it up to you.

And later, when you look back, it will become increasingly clear to you that you made the right choice in following Him. You'll realize not only that God has made it up to you in this life, but also that He'll make it up to you in eternity when you hear Him say, "Well done, good and faithful servant" (Matthew 25:21).

THE LORD'S INVITATION TO HIS PEOPLE

Seek first the kingdom of God and
His righteousness, and all these things
shall be added to you.

JESUS, IN MATTHEW 6:33

WITH GOD IN PRAYER

Acknowledge His ownership of everything in your life and His right to ask you to let go of anything.

MOVE BEYOND A SENSE OF LOSS

Evaluate your life and the things that fill it up. Is God asking you to give up anything?

Your own reflections...personal application... personal prayer points...

Powered
by His Spirit

When we think of being filled with the Spirit, we often relate it to an emotional experience or a feeling of euphoria. But in reality, when God tells us to "be filled with the Spirit" (Ephesians 5:18), the word translated as "filled" could also be rendered as "controlled by." It's a word that speaks of what happens when the wind fills the sails of a boat and guides it along. So God is saying we're to let His Spirit fill us and control our lives.

Another interesting thing is that the tense of this word (in the original language) speaks of something that should be done continually. So we could translate it, "Be continually filled with the Spirit." It's not a one-time event. Instead, it's something taking place over and over again, just as we repeatedly fill the gas tanks in our cars to keep them running.

God wants to refill us with His Spirit continually. It's a great thing to say each day, *Lord, fill me with Your Spirit. Lord, fill me once again.*

> If you **sinful** people know how to give **good** gifts to your children, how much more will your heavenly Father **give** the Holy Spirit to those who ask him.
> JESUS, IN LUKE 11:13 NLT

You may have emotional experiences. You may not have emotional experiences. But that has little to do with the reality of being filled with and controlled by the Spirit.

One other thing not to miss about this phrase from Ephesians 5:18 is that it's a command, not a suggestion. The Scripture isn't saying, "If it works with your schedule, if you don't mind, would you please consider maybe letting the Holy Spirit fill and control you?" Rather, God is commanding us, ordering us, to be filled with the Holy Spirit.

THE LORD'S INVITATION TO HIS PEOPLE

Don't be drunk with wine,
because that will ruin your life.
Instead, be filled with the Holy Spirit.
EPHESIANS 5:18 NLT

WITH GOD IN PRAYER

Give Him praise and thanks for the wonderful gift of His Spirit. And say to Him, "Lord, fill me with Your Spirit. Lord, fill me once again."

MOVE BEYOND A LACK OF SPIRITUAL POWER

Think about this: How do you know when you are filled with the Spirit? How do you know when you're not? Evaluate yourself honestly, so you can always bring your true condition before God in prayer.

Your own reflections...personal application... personal prayer points...

Thankful in Everything

In her wonderful book *The Hiding Place,* Corrie ten Boom relates an amazing story about the importance of being thankful. Corrie and her sister, Betsy, were held in a concentration camp known as Ravensbrück, where they lived in barracks plagued with lice. Lice were everywhere—in their hair and on their bodies. One day Betsy said to her, "Corrie, we need to give thanks to God for the lice."

Corrie said, "Betsy, you've gone too far this time. I'm not going to thank God for lice."

Betsy said, "Oh, but Corrie, the Bible tells us, 'In everything give thanks.' "

Still, Corrie didn't want to thank God for the lice. As it turns out, Corrie and Betsy were trying to reach the other women in their barracks with the message of the gospel, and they'd been holding Bible studies. Corrie found out later that because of the lice, the guards wouldn't go into those barracks, and therefore, they were able to have their Bible studies. As a result, they led many of the women to the Lord. So it turns out God can even use lice.

> In everything give **thanks**; for this is
> the will of God in Christ Jesus for you.
> 1 THESSALONIANS 5:18

If the Bible said, "In some things give thanks," I would say, "No problem there!" But it says, "In everything give thanks." That isn't an easy thing to do.

This verse doesn't say we should give thanks *for* everything as much as it says *in* everything. There are some things that happen, and I'm not glad they happened. But I'm glad that, in spite of the tragedies, God is still on the throne, and He's still in control of all circumstances surrounding my life.

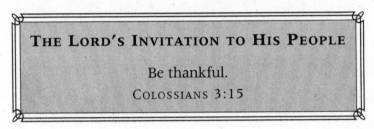

THE LORD'S INVITATION TO HIS PEOPLE

Be thankful.

COLOSSIANS 3:15

WITH GOD IN PRAYER

Take plenty of time today to express your thanksgiving to Him for the grace and blessings He pours into your life.

MOVE BEYOND INGRATITUDE

When you fail to be grateful, how does it impact your attitudes and actions? Assess your life honestly in this area.

Your own reflections...personal application... personal prayer points...

To Know His Will

We find a conditional promise in Romans 12:1–2:

> I beseech you therefore, brethren, by the mercies of God, that you present your bodies a living sacrifice, holy, acceptable to God, which is your reasonable service. And do not be conformed to this world, but be transformed by the renewing of your mind, that you may prove what is that good and acceptable and perfect will of God.

In this passage the promise is that you can know what the perfect will of God is for your life. The conditions are that you must present yourself to God, and you must not be conformed to this world.

Notice the order. First, you offer yourself as a living sacrifice, and then you'll know the will of God. We tend to want to know God's will first and then decide whether we want to give ourselves to it.

It reminds me of when my son Jonathan was little. My wife would ask him, "Are you hungry?"

Often the response was, "What are you cooking?" If it was vegetables, he wasn't hungry at that particular moment. But if it was cookies, he was starving.

In the same way, we'll sometimes say, *Lord, what is your will? Before I'm going to surrender to it, I would like to know what I'm getting myself into.* But God may tell you something you don't want to hear. So the real question is, are you going to do what He says?

It has been said that the condition of an enlightened mind is a surrendered heart. If you want to know the will of God, you must have a heart that's surrendered. Present yourself to Him. Then accept His will, no matter what.

> ## THE LORD'S INVITATION TO HIS PEOPLE
>
> Dear brothers and sisters, I plead with you
> to give your bodies to God because of all he
> has done for you. Let them be a living and holy
> sacrifice—the kind he will find acceptable.
> This is truly the way to worship him.
>
> ROMANS 12:1 NLT

WITH GOD IN PRAYER

Surrender your heart to Him and present your whole life to Him.

MOVE BEYOND IGNORANCE OF GOD'S WILL

What is God showing you about His will for you? Is there something He's asking you to do that you're resisting? Honestly evaluate your heart on this issue and confess and forsake any resistance you discover.

Your own reflections...personal application... personal prayer points...

Taste and See

We need to remember that God's will is good. It may not seem like it at times, but it is. His plan for us is good. However, He usually doesn't give us a detailed blueprint of His will. Usually, God reveals it to us in bits and pieces. He sees the full picture, while we see only a little at a time.

If you had been Jacob, the father of Joseph in the Old Testament, you surely would have prayed for the welfare of your child. But when Joseph disappeared (after his own brothers secretly sold him into slavery), you could easily have protested, "God, what are You doing? Why did You allow this?" Yet if God hadn't allowed this to happen, Joseph never would have been put into a position of influence enabling him to save the country and his own family.

If you had been the mother of Moses, how your heart would have broken when you saw your own child being taken into Pharaoh's court! Yet it was all part of God's plan to mold Moses into a leader who would lead Israel out of Egypt and its bondage.

> He is the Rock; his deeds are perfect.
> Everything he does is just and **fair**.
> He is a **faithful** God who does no
> wrong; how just and **upright** he is!
> DEUTERONOMY 32:4 NLT

If you had been the mother of Jesus and watched your own son hanging on the cross, how easily you could have said, "Lord, why did You let this happen?" But if Jesus hadn't died on that cross and taken our sins upon Himself, we could never know eternal life.

So when you look at the will of God in progress, it may not always make sense. But you must believe God knows what He's doing. His will is good. Just wait until He finishes what He has begun.

THE LORD'S INVITATION TO HIS PEOPLE

Taste and see that the LORD is good.
Oh, the joys of those who take refuge in him!
PSALM 34:8 NLT

WITH GOD IN PRAYER

Give thanks to Him that His will is always good.

MOVE BEYOND DISSATISFACTION
WITH GOD'S WILL

What specific actions can you pursue today that you know are God's will?

Your own reflections...personal application... personal prayer points...

Sibling Rivalry

I think there may be three big surprises for us in heaven: One, many of the people we expected to see won't be there. Two, many of the people we never expected to see will be there. And three, we will be there.

Remember the story of the prodigal son? He went out, tarnished the family name, consorted with prostitutes, and threw away his fortune. Then one day he came to his senses and returned home. His father ran to meet him, smothered him with kisses, and threw a big party. It was a great celebration.

Meanwhile, the prodigal's older brother was out in the field. Hearing the commotion, he wanted to know what was going on. He was told his younger brother had just returned home. But instead of rejoicing, he was angry and jealous.

> If one part suffers, all the parts
> suffer with it, and if one **part** is
> honored, all the parts are glad. All
> of you together are Christ's **body**,
> and **each** of you is a part of it.
> 1 CORINTHIANS 12:26-27 NLT

This can happen with us. We see God bless another Christian in a tangible way, maybe with a promotion at work or another blessing of some kind. Our reaction is to think how we were more deserving of that blessing.

Or maybe God puts His hand on a certain individual and begins to use that person in a remarkable way. Then we say, *Lord, wait a second. I've faith-*

fully served You all these years. How is it this Johnny-come-lately pops up, and You're blessing him? It isn't fair. I'm much more godly. I'm much more committed. And most of all, I'm much more humble.

The truth is that we should rejoice whenever God is being glorified and the gospel is being preached. In God's family, there's no room for sibling rivalry.

THE LORD'S INVITATION TO HIS PEOPLE

Rejoice with those who rejoice.

ROMANS 12:15

WITH GOD IN PRAYER

Give Him praise and thanks for the many surprising ways He accomplishes His work and purpose. Thank Him especially for His grace that's so evident in the surprising ways that He blesses and uses people.

MOVE BEYOND SPIRITUAL JEALOUSY

If you've had the wrong attitude toward someone who's experienced God's blessing, confess this and move beyond it at once.

Your own reflections...personal application... personal prayer points...

God's Fellow Workers

In 1 Samuel 30, we find the story of David and his soldiers returning home with the spoils of a successful battle. They were met by those who had stayed behind to guard the camp and the army's supplies. Then some of the soldiers who fought in the battle announced that they wouldn't give any of the spoils to those who stayed by the camp.

I love David's response: "As his part is who goes down to the battle, so shall his part be who stays by the supplies; they shall share alike" (1 Samuel 30:24).

Maybe God has called you to serve Him in such a way that people easily see what you're doing. Or He may have called you to serve Him by staying in the background while supporting others who are seen. Either way, God will bless you and reward you in that final day.

Maybe you feel as though your life isn't really making a difference, or you think what you have to offer God doesn't mean all that much. You'll be in for some surprises in heaven, because what may not seem valuable on earth will be of great value in heaven.

> He who **plants** and he who waters are one, and each one will **receive** his own reward according to his own labor.
> 1 CORINTHIANS 3:8

I read a story about a man who found an old blue and white vase while he was cleaning his attic. He took it to an auction to sell it, thinking he would probably get twenty or thirty dollars for it. To his amazement, the vase sold for $324,000. It was an original fifteenth-century Chinese vase from the Ming dynasty.

What may not seem valuable now will be later. Until then, we need to be faithful with what God has given us to do.

> ## THE LORD'S INVITATION TO HIS PEOPLE
>
> Be faithful until death,
> and I will give you the crown of life.
> REVELATION 2:10

WITH GOD IN PRAYER

Thank Him for the specific calling and responsibilities He has given you.

MOVE BEYOND UNFAITHFULNESS

What specific responsibilities has God set before you today? Make the commitment to be faithful in those responsibilities...and then carry them out.

Your own reflections...personal application... personal prayer points...

No Other Gods

When God gave the Ten Commandments, He began by saying we should have no other gods before Him or make any idol for ourselves. That means we're not to allow anything or anyone to take God's place in our lives. The Bible tells us, "Dear children, keep away from anything that might take God's place in your hearts" (1 John 5:21 NLT).

> You must not have any other god but me.
> You must not make for yourself an **idol** of
> any kind.… You must not **bow** down to them
> or worship them, for I, the LORD your God,
> am a **jealous** God who will not tolerate
> your affection for **any** other gods.
>
> EXODUS 20:3-5 NLT

Scripture warns us about idols that include objects or carved images. Before we dismiss this as an issue from the Old Testament period, let's consider how many religious icons and images we have in our culture today. While I'm not saying all of these are necessarily wrong, I'm saying we don't need them to worship God.

Sometimes people say, "I need these things to remind me of God." But a person who knows God, loves Him, and is living in fellowship with Him does not need an image or a representation of God to worship Him. A dependence on such things indicates the absence of a vital inner spiritual life. Jesus said,

"God is Spirit, so those who worship him must worship in spirit and in truth" (John 4:24 NLT).

We don't need images. We don't need icons. We don't need symbols. God tells us, "Do not make idols of any kind." Give Him your undivided love.

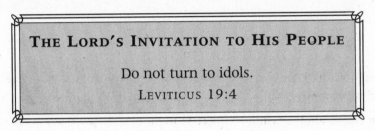

THE LORD'S INVITATION TO HIS PEOPLE

Do not turn to idols.

LEVITICUS 19:4

WITH GOD IN PRAYER

Worship Him with all your heart, soul, mind, and strength.

MOVE BEYOND IDOLATRY

Have you been drawn to any kind of "images" that violate the Lord's command? If so, confess this, and turn away from them.

Your own reflections...personal application... personal prayer points...

He Walked Among Us

One thing throughout the centuries that has fascinated people, especially artists, is the question of what Jesus looked like. It's interesting that no actual physical description of Jesus is found in Scripture, except for a figurative one in the book of Revelation. You would think that somewhere in one of the Gospels someone would have taken the time to give us just an idea of what He looked like: "Oh, by the way, Jesus was five foot eleven and had wavy, brownish hair and green eyes." But nothing like that is there.

> We do not look at the things which are seen,
> but at the **things** which are not seen.
> 2 Corinthians 4:18

Isaiah's prophecies about the Messiah indicate that He had a beard (see Isaiah 50:6) and that there was nothing in His physical appearance to make Him particularly attractive (see 53:2). We don't know anything more, so we can't accurately picture what He looked like. Do you wonder why that is?

I think perhaps it's because God knows our propensity for idol worship. So He left out of the Scriptures any physical description of Jesus, knowing we would end up worshiping His image and forgetting all about Him.

Quite honestly, I seriously doubt He looked like the Jesus so often depicted throughout history. I don't think Jesus had blond hair and piercing blue eyes. Being from the area in Israel that He was, His skin and hair would likely have been dark. His eyes would have been dark as well. But that isn't really important, is it?

God didn't give us a physical description of His Son. He wants us to focus on the greater reality of who Jesus was and is—the Son of God and God the Son, fully God and fully man.

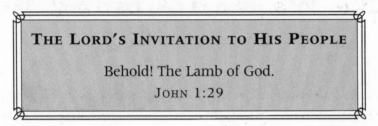

THE LORD'S INVITATION TO HIS PEOPLE

Behold! The Lamb of God.
JOHN 1:29

WITH GOD IN PRAYER

Praise Him for sending His Son into our world in bodily form. Give thanks to the Lord Jesus for sharing in your humanity so He could bear the punishment for your sins.

MOVE BEYOND IDOLATRY

Focus on the description of the risen and glorified Jesus Christ that was given to the apostle John (and to us!) in Revelation 1:12–16.

Your own reflections...personal application... personal prayer points...

No Idols

God commands us against having idols (see Exodus 20:3)—anything that takes the place of God in our lives. Idols can be a lot of things. Your career can be a rival to God. So can a possession. So can a relationship. An idol is any object, idea, philosophy, habit, occupation, sport, or whatever has one's primary concern and loyalty, or that to any degree decreases one's trust and loyalty to God.

Alan Redpath helps us understand idolatry: "Our god is the person we think is the most precious, for whom we would make the greatest sacrifice, who moves our hearts with the warmest love. He or it is the person who, if we lost him, would leave us desolate."

This definition really opens up the possibilities, doesn't it? A lot of things could qualify as idols in our lives. It's a true but terrifying fact that a person can attend church every Sunday and still be an idolater.

We all **know** that an idol is not really a god and that there is only one God. There may be so-called gods both in **heaven** and on earth, and some people actually worship many gods and many lords. But we know that there is only one God, the **Father**, who **created** everything, and we live for him. And there is only **one** Lord, Jesus Christ, **through** whom God made everything and through whom we have been **given** life.

1 CORINTHIANS 8:4-6 NLT

Is there one thing in your life that, if God asked you for it, you would say, *Absolutely not*? Is there one thing that, if the Lord required it of you, you would answer, *Anything but this*? If so, then maybe that thing, that pursuit, or that passion is an idol in your life.

Is there an idol in your heart today? Is there someone or something more precious to you than God Himself? Any person or pursuit that takes the place of God in your life will not satisfy. Let Him be your Lord. Let Him be your God. He will satisfy you.

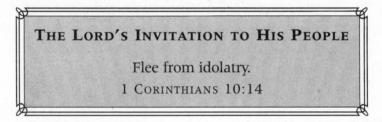

THE LORD'S INVITATION TO HIS PEOPLE

Flee from idolatry.
1 CORINTHIANS 10:14

WITH GOD IN PRAYER

Acknowledge His rightful authority to everything you are and have.

MOVE BEYOND IDOLATRY

If there is anything in your life that's a rival to God, let go of it today.

Your own reflections...personal application... personal prayer points...

Mean What You Say

One of the most obvious ways of taking the Lord's name in vain is through profanity. Unfortunately, most of us have heard the Lord's name taken in vain in that sense. That always bothers me because that's my Lord they're speaking of. We might even find ourselves correcting someone. "You shouldn't take the Lord's name in vain," we might say. And we'd be right.

> You shall not take the name of the LORD your God in vain, for the LORD will not hold him **guiltless** who takes His name in vain.
>
> EXODUS 20:7

But did you know that profanity isn't the only way to take His name in vain? The phrase "in vain" describes something empty, idle, insincere, and frivolous. Think about that. To take His name in vain means to use His name in an empty or idle or insincere or frivolous way.

As Christians, we often find ourselves tossing up little spiritual clichés such as "God bless you," "Praise the Lord," or, "I'll pray for you." There's nothing wrong with these statements, but if we say them, we should mean them. We shouldn't say, "Praise the Lord," or, "God bless you," when our hearts aren't really in it. When we tell people, "I'll pray for you," then we should pray for them. Otherwise, we shouldn't say it at all.

Jesus said, "Why do you call Me 'Lord, Lord,' and not do the things which I say?" (Luke 6:46). When we say He's our Lord yet don't do what He tells us to, that's the ultimate way of taking His name in vain.

Hypocrisy in the church is far worse than profanity in the street. Let's be careful not to take His name in vain.

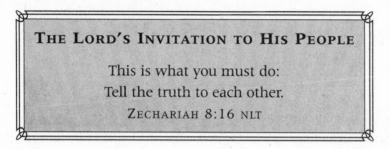

THE LORD'S INVITATION TO HIS PEOPLE

This is what you must do:
Tell the truth to each other.
ZECHARIAH 8:16 NLT

WITH GOD IN PRAYER

Fall to your knees and acknowledge the holiness of the Lord's name.

MOVE BEYOND TAKING THE LORD'S NAME IN VAIN

In what specific ways do you need to grow in being more faithful and pure in how you use the Lord's name?

Your own reflections...personal application... personal prayer points...

Remembering God

The Ten Commandments can be broken into two sections. The first four deal with our relationship with God, while the next six deal with our relationships with people.

In the commandments regarding our relationship with God, the final one pertains to the Sabbath. The Sabbath day was something set aside for God's people, a day in which they were to worship the Lord and rest from their labors. God was in essence telling them to keep this day as a holy day unto Him.

But I also believe the Sabbath day was pointing to something more than a twenty-four-hour period. In fact, the New Testament tells us, "There remains a Sabbath rest for the people of God, for whoever has entered God's rest has also rested from his works as God did from his" (Hebrews 4:9–10 ESV).

The rest the Sabbath pointed toward is a rest in our relationship with God in which we recognize we don't have to do things to earn His approval but have found His approval in what Christ has done for us.

> Remember to observe the Sabbath day by keeping it **holy**. You have six days each week for your ordinary work, but the seventh day is a **Sabbath** day of rest dedicated to the LORD your God.
> EXODUS 20:8-10 NLT

In our modern society where we work so hard for success, few people seem to take time off to remember God and to thank Him for all He has done for them. We seem to be too busy for God—until a crisis hits and we suddenly find time to ask for His help.

Let's be sure we're taking time to honor God and to thank Him for all He has done for us.

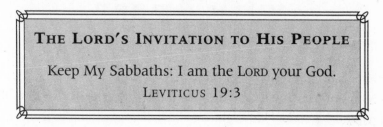

THE LORD'S INVITATION TO HIS PEOPLE

Keep My Sabbaths: I am the LORD your God.
LEVITICUS 19:3

WITH GOD IN PRAYER

Acknowledge God's wisdom in giving us the gift of the Sabbath.

MOVE BEYOND BEING TOO BUSY FOR GOD

Honestly evaluate your life on this issue: Are you pleasing God in how you use your time on the Sabbath day? Are you letting Him have the time that belongs to Him?

Your own reflections...personal application... personal prayer points...

The Problem with Anger

The sixth commandment obviously forbids the taking of another human life for no justifiable reason. We might say, "Well, I've never murdered anyone. At least I can say I haven't broken this commandment." But in the Sermon on the Mount, Jesus declared,

> You have heard that our ancestors were told, "You must not murder. If you commit murder, you are subject to judgment." But I say, if you are even angry with someone, you are subject to judgment! If you call someone an idiot, you are in danger of being brought before the court. And if you curse someone, you are in danger of the fires of hell. (Matthew 5:21–22 NLT)

So, anger in our hearts can be like murdering someone. "Anyone who hates another brother or sister is really a murderer at heart. And you know that murderers don't have eternal life within them" (1 John 3:15 NLT). The word translated here as "hate" means "to habitually despise." It's not speaking of only a passing emotion of the affections, but a deep-rooted loathing.

Now we all lose our tempers here and there. But this is speaking of hating, loathing, or despising someone. It's allowing bitterness toward someone to develop over a period of time—to the point that you're seething with anger every time you see that person or hear his or her name.

You must **not** murder.
EXODUS 20:13 NLT

Spreading lies about others, gossiping about them, or assassinating their characters can be like murder. If you love God, you'll love your neighbor. And if you love your neighbor, you won't do these things to them.

> ## THE LORD'S INVITATION TO HIS PEOPLE
>
> Walk worthy of the calling with which you were called...bearing with one another in love.
> EPHESIANS 4:1–2

WITH GOD IN PRAYER

Praise and thank God for creating human beings in His own image, and acknowledge before Him the sacredness and God-given dignity that belong to the life of every person you'll ever meet.

MOVE BEYOND ANGER AT OTHERS

Have you been guilty of anger toward someone? Confess this sin and turn away from it. If you expressed your anger in some way toward that person, go to him or her and ask for forgiveness.

Your own reflections...personal application... personal prayer points...

A Word to Children

The fifth of the Ten Commandments deals with the family but in essence establishes the foundation for how we're to treat our fellow human beings. The family provides the strength of our country today. It has been said that a family can survive without a nation, but a nation cannot survive without the family.

The Bible says, "Children, obey your parents because you belong to the Lord, for this is the right thing to do" (Ephesians 6:1 NLT). Why should children obey their parents? Because God says it's the right thing to do. That's all you need to know.

It's sort of like when you were growing up and would ask your mom or dad, "Why do I have to do this?"

"Because I said so."

"But I don't understand."

"I know. One day you will understand. But for now, it's just because I said so."

> Honor your father **and** your mother,
> that your **days** may be long upon the land
> which the LORD your God is **giving** you.
> EXODUS 20:12

What's right and what's wrong isn't based on what we think or on a consensus of what others think. Something is right because God says it's right. Something is wrong because God says it's wrong.

Needless to say, this flies against the cultural bias of today. Nowadays we hear more about children's rights than about their responsibilities. Not only are children expected to rebel, they're even encouraged to do so. However, this isn't God's plan.

There's a twofold promise (both in Deuteronomy 5:16 and Ephesians 6:3) associated with obeying your parents: First, "that it may be well with you," which promises a quality of life. Second, that "you may live long on the earth," which promises a quantity of life.

THE LORD'S INVITATION TO HIS PEOPLE

Children, obey your parents in the Lord,
for this is right. "Honor your father and mother,"
which is the first commandment with promise:
"that it may be well with you and
you may live long on the earth."

EPHESIANS 6:1–3

WITH GOD IN PRAYER

Thank Him for His wisdom in establishing parental authority for your family.

MOVE BEYOND DISOBEDIENCE TO PARENTS

If you are a parent, are your children fully aware of this command? Are they obeying it? If not, talk with them about it. Make them aware of this sin in their lives, their responsibility to God in this area, and the promised reward He gives for obedience.

Your own reflections...personal application... personal prayer points...

Vulnerable Places

The seventh commandment says we are not to commit adultery. Many people might say, "Well, I've never done that." But Jesus said in the Sermon on the Mount: "You have heard that it was said to those of old, 'You shall not commit adultery.' But I say to you that whoever looks at a woman to lust for her has already committed adultery with her in his heart" (Matthew 5:27–28). Of course, this applies to a woman as well, if she looks at a man lustfully.

This word Jesus used for "look" doesn't just mean a casual glance; in the original language it refers to the continuous act of looking. This is not an incidental or involuntary glance, but intentional and repeated gazing.

Jesus isn't speaking here of unexpected and unavoidable exposure to sexual temptation. He's speaking of someone who intentionally puts himself or herself into a vulnerable place. You understand the difference. We all live in a wicked world; tragically, we don't need to go far to see sexually explicit images. Television is one place. Then, of course, there's the Internet. Even if you've been careful to avoid these temptations in your home, when you walk into a mall or a store today, there'll be monitors playing videos, plus billboards and advertisements all around you. So we're constantly being exposed to sexual temptations.

> He has given us **great** and precious **promises**. These are the promises that enable you to share his divine **nature** and escape the world's corruption caused by human desires.
>
> 2 PETER 1:4 NLT

The person Jesus is describing who commits adultery in his or her heart is one who would intentionally put himself or herself into a place of obvious temptation. Those who love God and want to please Him will not do this.

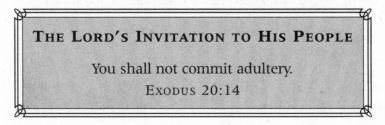

THE LORD'S INVITATION TO HIS PEOPLE

You shall not commit adultery.

EXODUS 20:14

WITH GOD IN PRAYER

Thank Him for His wisdom in requiring sexual purity in your body, in your thoughts, and in your words and actions.

MOVE BEYOND ADULTERY

Are you guilty of committing adultery in your mind? If so, confess this sin and repent of it. What specific help do you need to avoid this sin in the future?

Your own reflections...personal application... personal prayer points...

The Eighth Commandment

Stealing has become commonplace in our culture. We're so accustomed to people's stealing that we wouldn't even think of leaving our cars or homes unlocked. People break into cars. They break into houses. If you accidentally leave your wallet or purse somewhere, you don't ever expect to see it again. Stealing is so rampant in our culture that we're shocked when we see anyone being honest. It's such a rare quality today.

> You must **not** steal.
> EXODUS 20:15 NLT

Yet the temptation to steal is constant. When you sell that house or car, it's tempting to inflate the price a little. When you receive too much change, the temptation is to keep it.

But God says we should live honest lives. "If you are a thief, quit stealing. Instead, use your hands for good hard work, and then give generously to others in need" (Ephesians 4:28 NLT). The idea in this verse is not to simply cease doing what's wrong (stealing), but to start doing what's right, through honest work. The message is much the same in this verse: "Make it your ambition…to work with your hands, just as we told you, so that your daily life may win the respect of outsiders" (1 Thessalonians 4:11–12 NIV). And in this passage: "We hear that some of you are living idle lives, refusing to work.… We command such people and urge them in the name of the Lord Jesus Christ to settle down and work to earn their own living" (2 Thessalonians 3:11–12 NLT).

Know that God will honor the person who honors the principles of Scripture. The Bible tells us not to steal, and it means what it says. If you steal, you're unwise. And it will catch up with you.

THE LORD'S INVITATION TO HIS PEOPLE

Do not steal.
Do not deceive or cheat one another.
LEVITICUS 19:11 NLT

WITH GOD IN PRAYER

Thank Him for His wisdom in requiring total integrity in all that you are and do.

MOVE BEYOND STEALING

How can you ensure that you're fully and entirely honest in your work life and in the ways that you obtain possessions?

Your own reflections...personal application... personal prayer points...

Telling the Truth

Some years ago, a book called *The Day America Told the Truth* was published. According to the authors' findings, 91 percent of Americans lie on a regular basis. "The majority of us find it hard to go through a week without lying," the author states. "And one in five cannot make it throughout a single day without lying." Apparently, we're a lying culture.

While some people consciously lie, many others try to couch the truth with a little diplomacy because they don't want to offend someone. But God's Word has a lot to say about lying, and Proverbs 6 includes it in a list of things God hates. These include "a lying tongue" (verse 17) and "a false witness who speaks lies" (verse 19). From this, along with the ninth of the Ten Commandments ("You shall not bear false witness against your neighbor" [Exodus 20:16]), we can safely conclude that God hates lying.

> Lying lips are an **abomination** to the Lord.
> Proverbs 12:22

God is the source of all truth. Jesus said, "I am the way, the truth, and the life" (John 14:6 NLT). He's the embodiment of truth. Scripture also tells us it's impossible for God to lie (see Hebrews 6:18).

In dramatic contrast to this, Satan is described as "the father of lies" (John 8:44 NLT). So when we lie, we're behaving more like children of the devil than children of God.

THE LORD'S INVITATION TO HIS PEOPLE

Stop telling lies. Let us tell our neighbors
the truth, for we are all parts of the same body.
EPHESIANS 4:25 NLT

WITH GOD IN PRAYER

Praise Him for His truthfulness and for being the source of all truth. Acknowledge His hatred for falsehood and lies.

MOVE BEYOND FALSEHOOD

Are you guilty in some way of lying? If so, confess this sin and repent of it. What steps can you take to avoid this sin in the future?

Your own reflections...personal application... personal prayer points...

Contentment's Enemy

The tenth commandment, which forbids coveting, speaks to our deepest attitudes. Of course, the word *covet* means to be dissatisfied with what we have and to desire more, regardless of what it may cost us or someone else.

One Christmas when I was a young boy, I received everything I'd wanted. I was so happy. I thought, *This is the greatest Christmas I've ever had!* Then I went over to my friend's house and saw his gifts. Suddenly I was miserable, because he'd been given something I sort of wanted, but I'd forgotten about it. Suddenly the gifts I'd received (as wonderful as they were) were no longer acceptable, because my friend had something I wanted more.

That's what coveting is.

> True godliness with **contentment**
> is itself great wealth.
> 1 TIMOTHY 6:6 NLT

As adults, we can do this as well. We're content with what we have until we notice what somebody else has. Then we begin to covet that. We want it—and sadly, some will even go out and take whatever it is they're coveting. We might even covet another person's spouse. Coveting can ruin our lives.

Coveting is essentially greed, and it is not just a "little" sin. Jesus warns against it: "Take heed and beware of covetousness, for one's life does not consist in the abundance of the things he possesses" (Luke 12:15). The Bible says that covetousness is a form of idolatry (see Colossians 3:5). Paul even says this about covetousness: "Let it not even be named among you, as is fitting for saints" (Ephesians 5:3).

We are not to covet.

> ## THE LORD'S INVITATION TO HIS PEOPLE
>
> Let your conduct be without covetousness;
> be content with such things as you have.
> For He Himself has said, "I will
> never leave you nor forsake you."
> HEBREWS 13:5

WITH GOD IN PRAYER

Thank Him for all that He has given you.

MOVE BEYOND COVETING

Honestly evaluate your heart: Are you content with what you have?

Your own reflections...personal application... personal prayer points...

The Mother
Who Prayed

When we're praying for something we believe is the will of God, we should not give up. Keep asking, keep seeking, and keep knocking—that's what Jesus told us to do (see Matthew 7:7). In fact, when Jesus saw the great faith of a mother from Canaan who was doing this very thing, He gave her a blank check, so to speak: "Let it be to you as you desire" (Matthew 15:28).

This mother believed that her request (for her daughter to be healed) was God's will, and she wouldn't give up.

> Jesus **answered** and said to her,
> "O woman, great is your **faith**! Let
> it **be** to you as you desire." And her
> daughter was healed from that very hour.
> MATTHEW 15:28

Maybe you, like this mother, have a child who's under the devil's influence today. This child has rejected your influence, at least for now. It's tough, because you've raised your son or daughter in the ways of the Lord. The very thing you've prepared your child for—to become independent—has happened. My advice is: hold on and keep praying.

The situation in your child's life that looks like the worst-case scenario might just be a step toward bringing that child to a true, heartfelt faith. The rebellion may be difficult to endure right now. But it also may be short term, and it may be what it takes to bring your child to a place of realizing his or her own need for Jesus Christ.

Our kids need to get godly convictions in their hearts as their convictions, not just as Mom or Dad's convictions. It may mean a detour into the land of the prodigal. It may mean hitting bottom. But don't give up. Keep praying. Our children can escape our presence, but they cannot escape our prayers.

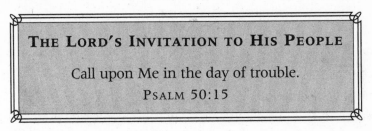

THE LORD'S INVITATION TO HIS PEOPLE

Call upon Me in the day of trouble.
PSALM 50:15

WITH GOD IN PRAYER

Bring before Him your own child (or any young person you know) who is not following the Lord. Ask God to be at work in that child's circumstances and heart to bring him or her to faith and humble submission to the Lord Jesus Christ.

MOVE BEYOND INADEQUATE PRAYER
FOR YOUR CHILDREN

Make specific plans for daily, concentrated prayer for your own child or any other young person who desperately needs this.

Your own reflections...personal application... personal prayer points...

God's Free Gift

Many years ago, I was given some free tickets to Disneyland. I was walking around the park, having a good time, but I started to feel guilty because I had two extra tickets.

Thinking there might be someone outside who wanted in and couldn't afford it, I decided to go find someone to give the tickets to. I noticed some kids hanging out in front of the park. I walked up and said, "Hi. I have two free tickets to Disneyland. Would you like them?"

"What are you doing, man?"

"Just two free tickets," I said.

"How much will it cost us?"

"It won't cost you anything. I have two extra tickets. I would just like you to have them."

"No."

> The wages of sin is **death**,
> but the gift of God is eternal
> **life** in Christ Jesus our Lord.
> ROMANS 6:23

I went to someone else. "Hi. I have these two free tickets to Disneyland. I would like to give them to you." Again and again, I received the same response. It took forty minutes to give away those tickets.

People are suspicious, and the same goes when it comes to spiritual things. We might say, "The way to be forgiven of your sin and to have eternal life is to turn from your sin, receive Jesus Christ into your heart as your Lord and Savior, and begin to follow Him." People respond, "That's too easy. What's the catch? What else do I have to do?"

In our pride, we want to think we have something to do with our salvation. But if we'll come to God on His terms and do what He says, we'll be forgiven of our sins and have the assurance of eternal life.

THE LORD'S INVITATION TO HIS PEOPLE

Yes, come, buy [priceless, spiritual] wine and milk without money and without price [simply for the self-surrender that accepts the blessing].

ISAIAH 55:1 AMP

WITH GOD IN PRAYER

Give thanks for His free gift of salvation to you through the death of Jesus Christ.

MOVE BEYOND PRIDEFUL SUSPICION OF GOD

Who can you talk with today about God's free gift of salvation? Who needs to hear the gospel?

Your own reflections...personal application... personal prayer points...

Speaking Up

Scripture tells us about Naaman, a commander of the Syrian army, who was loved by the people and by the king. He had everything a man could dream of, but he had one major problem. It was called leprosy.

So who did God use to reach this man? Did He send the prophet Elisha to come knocking at his door? Did God send an angel to reach him?

No. Instead, God sent a young Jewish girl who had been taken captive and had been carried away to Syria. How easily this girl could have been bitter against God for allowing this to happen. Yet she spoke to Naaman's wife about the prophet Elisha, and Naaman's wife in turn spoke to Naaman. He made the trip to see Elisha, who gave him a rather peculiar prescription, and Naaman was healed that very day.

> And the Syrians had gone out on raids, and had brought back captive a young **girl** from the land of Israel. She waited on Naaman's wife. Then she said to her mistress, "If only my **master** were with the prophet who is in Samaria! For he would **heal** him of his leprosy."
>
> 2 KINGS 5:2-3

Thank God for this girl who spoke up to Naaman's wife, who then told Naaman about the prophet in Israel. And thank God for every believer who speaks up in his or her home. Thank God for the believers who speak up in their schools and in their workplaces to tell people there's a God who can forgive sins.

People today are seeking. They're in search mode, especially as they see such an uncertain future in our world with all the rapid changes taking place around the globe. People are wondering what's going on. They're questioning the meaning of life.

And God's Word has the answers.

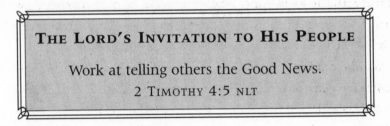

THE LORD'S INVITATION TO HIS PEOPLE

Work at telling others the Good News.
2 TIMOTHY 4:5 NLT

WITH GOD IN PRAYER

Thank Him for the gospel of Jesus Christ, which meets all your deepest needs.

MOVE BEYOND A LACK
OF USEFULNESS FOR THE GOSPEL

Whom do you know who should hear today the message of God's forgiveness in Christ Jesus? Make your plans to meet and speak with this person.

Your own reflections...personal application... personal prayer points...

True Change

During a visit to the Pacific Northwest a few years ago, I met a man who told me he'd been heavily into alcohol and drugs. He said his marriage had been hanging by a thread. One day he took a gun, loaded it, and was planning to kill himself. Then he turned on the television. There on the screen was a Harvest Crusade where I was sharing a message called, "How to Get Right with God."

"God began to speak to me," he told me. "When you led those people in prayer, I prayed and asked Jesus Christ to come into my life."

After he found Christ, he realized he needed to reconcile with his father. To see him, he rode his motorcycle across the country—and that's a long ride on a motorcycle.

That sounds like a conversion to me. That sounds like a man who had met God—there was a change in his life.

> If **anyone** is in Christ, he
> is a new creation; old things
> have passed away; **behold**,
> **all** things have become new.
> 2 CORINTHIANS 5:17

Throughout the Scriptures we see that a true encounter with God means change. For Naaman, healed of his leprosy, it meant wanting to show his gratitude with a gift. For Zacchaeus, it meant restoring what he'd stolen from others. For Saul, after seeing the Lord in a blinding light on the Damascus Road, it meant responding, "Lord, what do You want me to do?" (Acts 9:6). For the Philippian jailer who became a believer, it meant washing the backs of those he had previously whipped (see Acts 16:25–34).

If you've truly found a relationship with God through Jesus Christ, you'll change. That doesn't mean you need to change your life before you can come to Christ. But it does mean that after you come to Christ, you and your priorities will change.

THE LORD'S INVITATION TO HIS PEOPLE

Thus says the LORD of hosts…:
Amend your ways and your deeds.
JEREMIAH 7:3 ESV

WITH GOD IN PRAYER

Ask Him to show you the ways in which your life right now needs to change.

MOVE BEYOND FAILURE TO CHANGE

What do you need to do differently? What specific steps of change does God want you to take today?

Your own reflections...personal application... personal prayer points...

The Good in Guilt

Sir Arthur Conan Doyle, author of the Sherlock Holmes stories, wanted to play a practical joke on his friends. So he sent a note to twelve of them that simply read, "Flee at once. All is discovered." Within twenty-four hours, all twelve had left the country.

That's what you call a guilty conscience!

> Everyone has sinned; we all fall short of God's glorious standard. Yet God, with **undeserved** kindness, declares that we are righteous. He **did** this through Christ Jesus when he freed us from the **penalty** for our sins.
>
> ROMANS 3:23-24 NLT

If you ask me, I think we could use a little more guilt in our society. Guilt does serve a purpose. What good can possibly come from guilt? The same good that comes from the warning system in our bodies called pain. If you step on a piece of glass, your body sends a warning signal: "Stop! Don't go any farther!" In the same way, God has installed a warning system called guilt into our souls, and we experience it when we do something wrong.

Just as pain tells us there's a physical problem that must be dealt with or the body will suffer, guilt tells us something is wrong spiritually and needs to be confronted and cleansed.

So you see, guilt isn't necessarily a bad thing. The guilt feeling we experience is the symptom of the real problem, which is sin. All the psychological counseling in the world cannot relieve a person of his or her guilt. We can pretend it isn't there or try to find someone else to blame for our problems. But the only real and effective way to remove our guilt is to get to the root of the problem, which is sin.

THE LORD'S INVITATION TO HIS PEOPLE

Only acknowledge your guilt.
Admit that you rebelled against
the LORD your God.
JEREMIAH 3:13 NLT

WITH GOD IN PRAYER

Thank Him for the gift of your conscience and for how He uses guilt to help you want to turn from sin.

MOVE BEYOND A FEAR OF GUILT

If you're experiencing guilt, what must you do today to turn from the sin the Lord is convicting you of?

Your own reflections...personal application... personal prayer points...

The Search for God

Often we hear people say things such as, "I'm on a spiritual journey," "I'm trying to find the truth," "I'm trying to find the light," "I'm trying to find God," or, "I'm searching for Him."

Yet the Bible says that on our own none of us is really searching for Him: "No one is truly wise; no one is seeking God" (Romans 3:11 NLT). You would think that with all the religious belief systems in the world, this could simply not be. But

> The LORD looks **down** from heaven
> on the entire human race; he looks
> to see if anyone is truly **wise**, if
> anyone **seeks** God. But no, all have
> turned away; all have become corrupt.
> No one **does** good, not a single one!
> PSALM 14:2-3 NLT

God also plainly declares in His Word, "If you look for me wholeheartedly, you will find me" (Jeremiah 29:13 NLT). Let me be blunt: If you're truly seeking God, you'll find your way to Jesus Christ. And if you don't find your way to Jesus Christ, then you weren't really seeking God. You might be playing religious games. You might be dabbling with various belief systems. But the true seeker will find the true God, and those who claim to be true seekers, yet reject Jesus Christ, are not being honest with God or with themselves.

Religion is humanity's search for God; Christianity is God's search for humanity.

I've heard people say, "I found the Lord ten years ago," as though God had been lost. But God wasn't lost; we were. God is seeking to save us, and if we really want to know Him, then we'll find Him.

People resist coming to Jesus Christ because they bristle at the thought of being called sinners. They're unwilling to accept God's assessment of them. They're unwilling to acknowledge their guilt. That just bothers them. Instead, they want to believe they can get to heaven by their own merit, by their own goodness, by their own deeds, and by their own search. But the Bible says that simply won't work.

THE LORD'S INVITATION TO HIS PEOPLE

Thus says the LORD...: "Seek Me and live."

AMOS 5:4

WITH GOD IN PRAYER

Pray for the people you know who are resisting the gospel, who don't want to acknowledge their sin, or who have their own ideas about how to obtain eternal life.

MOVE BEYOND EMPTY RELIGION

Do you know people who think of themselves as being on a spiritual journey? Make a plan for discussing the gospel with them, and ask for God to prepare their hearts for this.

Your own reflections...personal application... personal prayer points...

Fearing God

I think there was a time in history when God was misrepresented as a divine being who threw lightning bolts down from heaven on people who displeased Him. We've all heard derogatory references to fire-and-brimstone preaching.

But I don't think such a view of God is the problem today. We don't hear that much about preachers delivering fire-and-brimstone messages anymore.

What we do hear are messages about how we can be successful. We hear messages about how God will prosper us. But it's rare to hear about a holy God who wants us to repent of our sins and walk with Him. That isn't popular anymore.

> They have no **fear** of God at all.
> ROMANS 3:18 NLT

In a way, I think many people have "created" a new God, an all-loving, benign being who's hovering somewhere up in the universe. If that's your view of Him, I'm here to tell you that isn't the God of the Bible. That's a god of your own making.

Without question, the real God is a God of love who loves you deeply. But the real God is also holy. Therefore, not only should we love God, but we should fear Him too.

What I mean by "fearing God" is not necessarily to be afraid of Him. It's to have a respect for God, a reverence for Him. One of the best translations I've heard of the term "fearing God" is this: "A wholesome dread of displeasing Him."

I think this is lacking in the lives of many people today and, sadly, even in the lives of people in the church. While it's true that the God we'll stand before one day is a God of love, it's also true that He's a holy God. So we need the fear of God.

THE LORD'S INVITATION TO HIS PEOPLE

Fear the LORD and turn away from evil.

PROVERBS 3:7 NLT

WITH GOD IN PRAYER

Praise Him for His holiness. Acknowledge how right it is that you should fear Him.

MOVE BEYOND FAILURE TO FEAR GOD

Evaluate your heart on this issue: If you knew for sure that you had recently displeased God, how much would this bother you? Do you have "a wholesome dread of displeasing Him"? If not, why not?

Your own reflections...personal application... personal prayer points...

Justified

Justification is an often-used word in the Christian vocabulary that carries great meaning. It's a word that declares the rightness of something—not symbolically or potentially, but actually. The Bible says when I come to Christ and ask Him to forgive my sin, recognizing how He died in my place and took the penalty I should have taken, then I've been justified.

When I come to Christ and ask His forgiveness, He says, "You are justified." Through faith in Him, I can therefore claim this truth: "I've been justified"— that is, "just as if I'd never sinned."

It's an incredible truth to think about! Sometimes guilt from the past can plague you. The devil may whisper, "Do you remember what you did? Do you remember that sin you committed twenty-three years ago?" But you can say, "I am justified—in God's eyes, it's just as if it never happened."

Only God makes this possible. As the Bible says, "He has not dealt with us according to our sins, nor punished us according to our iniquities. For as the heavens are high above the earth, so great is His mercy toward those who fear Him; as far as the east is from the west, so far has He removed our transgressions from us" (Psalm 103:10–12). He's removed our sins as far as the east is from the west. That's a long way!

You were washed, you were **sanctified**,
you were justified in the name of the Lord
Jesus **Christ** and by the Spirit of our God.
1 CORINTHIANS 6:11 ESV

Corrie ten Boom used to say how God has taken our sin and thrown it into the sea of forgetfulness, then posted a sign that says, "No fishing allowed." Yes, you are justified. It's just as if your sin had never happened.

THE LORD'S INVITATION TO HIS PEOPLE

Do not be children in your thinking. Be infants in evil, but in your thinking be mature.
1 CORINTHIANS 14:20 ESV

WITH GOD IN PRAYER

Fully express your gratitude for the fact that by faith in Jesus Christ you stand justified before the holy God.

MOVE BEYOND AN INADEQUATE VIEW OF JUSTIFICATION

If you truly stand justified before God, what difference should this make in your everyday life?

Your own reflections...personal application... personal prayer points...

An Invitation to Rest

One December day I was on my way to New York and had a connection through Chicago. It was cold outside, and as I was walking through the airport terminal, I noticed a large advertisement. It featured a sunny, tropical beach with beautiful, turquoise blue water, white sand, and an empty beach chair. That picture was so alluring and so appealing because of where I was at that particular moment.

I think that photograph represented something all of us really want—rest, relaxation, and time off. Jesus has something to say to the person who's exhausted and worn out. He has something to say to people who have been chewed up and spit out by life—people who are frustrated, hurting. Here's His personal offer of rest to those who will respond:

> Come to me, all of you who are weary and carry heavy burdens, and I
> will give you rest. Take my yoke upon you. Let me teach you, because I
> am humble and gentle at heart, and you will find rest for your souls.
> For my yoke is easy to bear, and the burden I give you is light.
> (Matthew 11:28–30 NLT)

Here we really have the Christian life in a nutshell. Here we see what it is to come to Jesus, to know Jesus, and to walk with Jesus.

> Those the Father has given me will come
> to me, and I will **never reject** them.
> JESUS, IN JOHN 6:37 NLT

This invitation stands today, but it won't stay that way forever. By this I mean that we don't know when our lives on this earth will end. In addition to this, there is the issue of hardening one's heart to something he has heard over and over again. The Bible says, "If you will hear His voice, do not harden your hearts" (Hebrews 4:7). This is simply not something you want to put off.

Jesus says, "Come to Me." That's it. It's so simple, yet so profound. And we see this same invitation echoed throughout Scripture. "The Spirit and the bride say, 'Come!' And let him who hears say, 'Come!' Whoever is thirsty, let him come; and whoever wishes, let him take the free gift of the water of life" (Revelation 22:17 NIV).

THE LORD'S INVITATION TO HIS PEOPLE

Jesus stood up and cried out,
saying, "If anyone thirsts,
let him come to Me and drink."
JOHN 7:37

WITH GOD IN PRAYER

If you feel weary or frustrated or weighed down by burdens, talk about this with the Lord, and let Him know that you fully accept His invitation to come to Him for rest.

MOVE BEYOND WEARINESS AND FRUSTRATION

If you feel weary or frustrated or burdened, what are the reasons for this? Are there changes that the Lord wants you to make in the way you handle life's pressures?

Your own reflections...personal application... personal prayer points...

The Two-Part Invitation

In Matthew 11, after Jesus promises to give rest to those who come to Him, He immediately follows those words with this invitation: "Take My yoke upon you and learn from Me" (verse 29). He's telling us there's more; His invitation to rest is a package deal. If we're true followers of Jesus Christ, we'll take not only his rest but also His yoke upon us.

But what does that mean?

The concept of a yoke would have been readily understood by the people of Jesus's day. It was a steering device placed on animals to guide the plows or carts they were pulling. So Jesus, in essence, is saying, "Take my steering device upon you." He's saying, "Let Me be in control of your life. Let Me guide your life. Let Me direct your life."

> My yoke is **easy** to bear, and
> the burden I give you is **light**.
> JESUS, IN MATTHEW 11:30 NLT

You might be thinking, "First Jesus says He'll give me rest, but then He says to put on His yoke. That sounds like work." I want you to know it will only be as much of a weight to you as wings are to a bird. It will be a joy, because now, instead of wasting your life serving yourself or living for pleasure or success or whatever else one lives for, you'll be channeling your energies into following and serving Jesus Christ.

You may give up some things to follow the Lord. But what you give up can't begin to compare to what He has given and will give you. It isn't just a great thing to do with your life. It's the most satisfying thing to do with your life.

> ## THE LORD'S INVITATION TO HIS PEOPLE
>
> Take my yoke upon you. Let me teach you,
> because I am humble and gentle at heart,
> and you will find rest for your souls.
> JESUS, IN MATTHEW 11:29 NLT

WITH GOD IN PRAYER

Thank the Lord for the unsurpassed privilege of bearing His yoke.

MOVE BEYOND WASTING YOUR LIFE

What do you need to do now to channel more of your energies into following and serving Jesus Christ?

Your own reflections...personal application... personal prayer points...

Clothed
with Christ

I like comfortable clothes. Most of the time you'll find me wearing jeans, because they're comfortable. I don't like starched shirts, and when I send my shirts to the cleaners, I specify "no starch."

For some reason, at one of the cleaners we previously used, "no starch" meant "extra starch." I would put on one of these shirts and could barely move in it, it was so stiff. That isn't the kind of clothing I want. I want clothes that move when I move.

This catches the meaning behind the phrase in Romans 13:14, "put on the Lord Jesus Christ." It means to enter into His views and His interests and to imitate Him in all things.

> All who have been **united** with **Christ** in baptism have put on Christ, like putting on new clothes.
> GALATIANS 3:27 NLT

To "put on the Lord Jesus" denotes the same concept as a person's putting on clothing. It's the idea of letting Jesus Christ be a part of every aspect of your life. Let Him be with you when you get up in the morning. Make Him a part of your life today, going with you everywhere, and acting through you in everything you do.

J. B. Phillips paraphrases that verse in this way: "Let us be Christ's men from head to foot." I like that. Too often we're on a collision course with God, fighting Him and resisting Him. Too often, instead of going where God wants us to go and doing what He wants us to do, we're pulling against Him at every turn. When this is the case, we lose—we lose big.

So why fight it? Recognize that His plan for you is better than the plan you have for yourself.

THE LORD'S INVITATION TO HIS PEOPLE

Put on the Lord Jesus Christ, and make no provision for the flesh, to fulfill its lusts.
ROMANS 13:14

WITH GOD IN PRAYER

Talk to God about your desire to have Jesus Christ be a part of every aspect of your life.

MOVE BEYOND PULLING AGAINST CHRIST

Is there any area of life in which you're pulling against the Lord instead of going along with Him? Identify this and make the changes He wants you to make.

Your own reflections...personal application... personal prayer points...

Remembering to Say "Thank You"

In the Old Testament we find an interesting story of how King Jehoshaphat took an uncommon approach when his enemies waged war against him. Instead of sending in his army first, he sent in the choir and musicians.

Imagine the scene: "All right, guys, here's the plan today. An army is out there, armed to the teeth. So we're sending in the choir and the musicians."

If I'd been a choir member or musician, I might have wondered whether the king liked our music. But God had directed Jehoshaphat in this unusual battle tactic. We read that Jehoshaphat appointed people to sing to the Lord, praise the beauty of holiness, and go out in front of the army saying, "Praise the LORD, for His mercy endures forever" (2 Chronicles 20:21).

> Oh, that men would give thanks to the
> LORD for His **goodness**, and for His
> wonderful works to the children of men!
> PSALM 107:8

So that's exactly what they did. The Bible tells us that when they began to sing and praise, God sent an ambush against the enemy, and they were destroyed. God's people were able to go into this situation giving thanks, because He was in control.

In approaching God to ask for new blessings, we should never forget to thank Him for the blessings He has already given. Have you recently come to God for help and He came through for you? Did you come back to say "thank you"? If we would stop and think how many of the prayers we've offered to God have been answered and how seldom we come back to God to thank Him, it just might amaze—and embarrass—us. We should be just as deliberate in giving thanks to God as we are in asking for His help.

THE LORD'S INVITATION TO HIS PEOPLE

Enter into His gates with thanksgiving,
and into His courts with praise.
Be thankful to Him, and bless His name.
PSALM 100:4

WITH GOD IN PRAYER

Honor Him today by taking time to express gratitude for His blessings to you and for His answers to your prayers. Be specific in naming them and being thankful for them.

MOVE BEYOND UNGRATEFULNESS

How can you be more deliberate and purposeful in thanking God daily?

Your own reflections...personal application... personal prayer points...

When Storms Come

At the conclusion of Matthew 7, Jesus told the story of two men who built two types of houses. One house was built on a good foundation of rock, while the other was built on a faulty foundation of sand.

Then Jesus described a storm that came and beat against both houses. The house built on sand collapsed, while the house built on the rock stood firm. Jesus concluded that the man who built on the rock represents someone who hears the Word of God and obeys it. He said the man who built his house on sand is someone who hears the Word of God yet doesn't obey it.

In this story, notice that the storm struck both houses. Every life and every person will experience hardships. So the question is, How will you react when life's storms hit? Will they destroy you or strengthen you? Will they make you better...or bitter?

> No **chastening** seems to be joyful for the present, but painful; nevertheless, afterward it yields the peaceable fruit of **righteousness** to those who have been trained by it.
> HEBREWS 12:11

Here's the good news for Christians: we know that whatever happens in our lives must first go through the protective screen of God's love. In other words, God will not let anything happen in the life of a believer that He isn't completely aware of. The word *oops* is not in God's vocabulary. He's in full control of all the circumstances surrounding the lives of His people.

So when hardship comes, we know God has allowed it for a purpose. He has some plan in mind.

> ## THE LORD'S INVITATION TO HIS PEOPLE
>
> Do not fear any of those
> things which you are about to suffer.
> REVELATION 2:10

WITH GOD IN PRAYER

Thank Him for being in full control of all the circumstances in your life.

MOVE BEYOND LACK OF FAITH IN GOD'S CONTROL

How do you react when life's storms hit? Do hardships cause you to doubt God's wisdom and love for you? If so, why is this? What are you failing to remember?

Your own reflections...personal application... personal prayer points...

God's Answer
to Worry

In the Sermon on the Mount, Jesus had specific things to say about worry and anxiety:

> I tell you not to worry about everyday life—whether you have enough food and drink, or enough clothes to wear. Isn't life more than food, and your body more than clothing? Look at the birds. They don't plant or harvest or store food in barns, for your heavenly Father feeds them. And aren't you far more valuable to him than they are? Can all your worries add a single moment to your life? (Matthew 6:25–27 NLT)

Why should we not worry? First of all, Jesus tells us, because our heavenly Father is watching out for us. Jesus points to the birds. You've never seen a bird sweat, have you? Birds are relatively calm. Certainly, the birds need to go out and gather their food. They do their part to get what they need. But they don't worry about it. The point Jesus is making is that if God cares for the birds, won't He also take care of you? The answer obviously is yes, He will.

Second, Jesus reminds us that worry doesn't bring about anything productive in your life. It's a destructive emotion. It doesn't lengthen your life and can even potentially shorten it.

> Martha, Martha, you are **worried**
> and troubled about many things.
> JESUS, IN LUKE 10:41

The next time you're tempted to worry about something, channel all the energy you would have put into worry into prayer instead. Say, *Lord, here's my problem. I'm putting it in Your hands. I'm going to trust You.* That's not an easy thing to do. But it's something we need to consciously do.

> ## THE LORD'S INVITATION TO HIS PEOPLE
>
> Don't worry about anything; instead,
> pray about everything. Tell God what you need,
> and thank him for all he has done.
> PHILIPPIANS 4:6 NLT

WITH GOD IN PRAYER

Thank Him for how much He loves you and cares for you. And acknowledge before Him the destructiveness of worry.

MOVE BEYOND WORRY

Is anything causing you anxiety at this time? If so, what is it? Bring this issue to the Lord, put it into His hands, and acknowledge your trust in Him to take care of it.

Your own reflections...personal application... personal prayer points...

Time Will Tell

After God called Gideon to deliver His people from their Midianite oppressors, Gideon quickly raised a fairly large army of thirty-two thousand men, which was good, because he faced a much larger adversary. In the enemy's camp, the Midianites and their allies were "as numerous as locusts; and their camels were without number, as the sand by the seashore in multitude" (Judges 7:12).

But God came to Gideon and told him his army was too big. He told Gideon to send home any of the soldiers who were timid or afraid. Gideon obeyed the Lord, and twenty-two thousand men responded, "We're out of here." Then God thinned the ranks even more, leaving only three hundred men. He told Gideon, "With these 300 men I will rescue you and give you victory over the Midianites. Send all the others home" (Judges 7:7 NLT).

Why did God do that? He was looking for those who would stand up for Him, for those who would make a sacrifice.

In the same way, time will tell whether you're a true follower of Jesus Christ. It will be determined on the battlefield, not in a church service where everyone's praising the Lord together. Time will tell whether you've truly gone forward spiritually. The true test will be how you hold up when the first difficulties come, when the first temptations come, and when the first persecution comes.

> You will be hated by all
> for My name's **sake**. But he who
> **endures** to the end will be saved.
> JESUS, IN MATTHEW 10:22

I remember how things changed when I became a follower of Jesus Christ. Friends whom I'd known for many years began to harass and mock me. I recognized immediately that if I followed Christ, I would lose some so-called friends, and this wouldn't always be easy.

If you're willing to endure, you'll have the greatest adventure imaginable in serving the Lord. God is looking for men and women to enlist in His army as His divine special forces.

THE LORD'S INVITATION TO HIS PEOPLE

You therefore must endure hardship
as a good soldier of Jesus Christ.

2 TIMOTHY 2:3

WITH GOD IN PRAYER

Ask Him to do whatever it takes to build up your spiritual endurance.

MOVE BEYOND A LACK OF ENDURANCE

When you've faced difficulties, temptations, or persecution, how have you responded?

Your own reflections...personal application... personal prayer points...

In His Strength

Just as police officers call for backup when they sense imminent danger, the first thing we must realize about spiritual battle is that in our own strength we're no match for the devil.

I think a healthier respect of the Adversary is in order for believers today. We don't want to underestimate Satan, nor do we want to overestimate him; we want to accurately assess who he is and what his abilities are. We need to recognize that he's powerful; we don't want to try and take him down in our own strength.

I hear some preachers on television or the radio calling the devil silly little names, laughing at him, or making jokes about him. But the Bible says that even the archangel Michael did not dare to condemn the devil with mockery. "Michael the archangel, in contending with the devil…dared not bring against him a reviling accusation, but said, 'The Lord rebuke you!' " (Jude 9). Michael let God do the rebuking. Michael had a healthy respect for the enemy's power.

> These people are proud and **arrogant**,
> daring even to scoff at supernatural
> beings **without** so much as trembling.
>
> 2 PETER 2:10 NLT

We need to "be strong in the Lord and in the power of His might" (Ephesians 6:10). It's our power base. Satan wants to separate us from God, because the moment he gets us away from Him, we're open prey. Thus, the devil wants to put a wedge between God and us.

The only power that can effectively drive Satan out is the power of Jesus Christ. Be strong in the Lord. Stay close to Him. Don't let anything come between you and God.

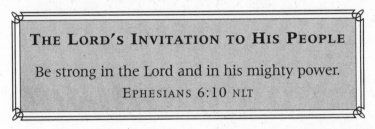

THE LORD'S INVITATION TO HIS PEOPLE

Be strong in the Lord and in his mighty power.
EPHESIANS 6:10 NLT

WITH GOD IN PRAYER

Praise Him for His mighty power and His eternal victory over Satan.

MOVE BEYOND OVERCONFIDENCE IN SPIRITUAL WARFARE

Are you convinced of your need for the Lord's help in resisting the devil and his power? In what ways have you failed to depend on the Lord's help in this area?

Your own reflections...personal application... personal prayer points...

Safe with the Son

I want to address a popular doctrine that has been floating around in the church for several years. Some have actually made theology out of what I believe is a false assumption.

There are people today who will tell you the reason you're having certain problems or struggling with certain vices and sins is because of a generational curse that's on you and your family. Maybe your father or grandfather or great-grandfather was involved in the occult, and therefore a generational curse has been passed on from them to you, which is why you're the way you are. Thus, according to this doctrine, you need to come against this generational curse by first identifying it and then rebuking it and finding out the specific demons that are a part of this curse.

It's all very interesting. But it isn't biblical. The Bible doesn't tell me to do these things. There's no "generational curse" on me, because that curse was broken on the day I gave my life to Jesus Christ. I'm not under any curse.

> We know that **God's children** do not make a practice of sinning, for God's Son holds them **securely**, and the evil one cannot touch them.
>
> 1 JOHN 5:18 NLT

Satan, however, is under the curse. So I'm to stand in God's power and recognize, as 1 John 5:18 says, that God's Son holds me securely, and the evil one cannot get his hands on me. He cannot attach himself to me. No generational curses here. No demonic possession of a Christian here.

I'm under the protection of God Almighty. "So if the Son sets you free, you are truly free" (John 8:36 NLT).

THE LORD'S INVITATION TO HIS PEOPLE

Stand fast therefore in the liberty
by which Christ has made us free.
GALATIANS 5:1

WITH GOD IN PRAYER

Thank Him that you are not the victim of some generational curse. Thank Him that Jesus Christ has delivered you from bondage to Satan and to sin. Thank Him also that Satan, your enemy, is eternally cursed.

MOVE BEYOND MISUNDERSTANDING EVIL'S CURSE

Think about the fact that in Jesus Christ "you are truly free" (John 8:36 NLT). How does this freedom affect the way you live your life today?

Your own reflections...personal application... personal prayer points...

Enemy Tactics

The devil tends to use the same tactics over and over again. I suppose he operates by the old adage, "If it ain't broke, don't fix it." He has used these techniques, plans, and strategies since the Garden of Eden, and they've worked with great effect to bring down countless people. Therefore, he just keeps bringing them back, generation after generation.

That's the bad news. The good news is that we know what his tactics are, because they're clearly identified in the Bible. The devil is a dangerous wolf who sometimes disguises himself as a sheep. Sometimes he comes to us as an angel of light. Other times he roars like a lion, coming to us in all of his depravity and horror. But more often he comes like a snake. This is why we always need to be on guard.

> We would not be **outwitted** by Satan;
> for we are not ignorant of his designs.
> 2 CORINTHIANS 2:11 ESV

He'll tempt you and whisper, "Trust me on this. Go ahead and sin. You'll get away with it. No one will ever know." So you take the bait and fall into sin. Then the devil shouts, "What a hypocrite! Do you think God would ever hear your prayers? And don't even bother going to church!" Sadly, some people will listen to this, believe it, and be driven away.

Just remember, no matter what you've done, no matter what sin you've committed, God will always be ready to forgive you if you'll turn from that sin and return to Him. Don't let the devil isolate you from God's Word and God's people, because that's exactly what he's trying to do.

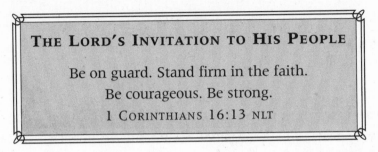

THE LORD'S INVITATION TO HIS PEOPLE

Be on guard. Stand firm in the faith.
Be courageous. Be strong.
1 CORINTHIANS 16:13 NLT

WITH GOD IN PRAYER

Ask Him to show you how you need to be on your guard against the devil's ways.

MOVE BEYOND IGNORANCE
OF THE DEVIL'S TACTICS

What should you do today to stay connected with God's Word and God's people?

Your own reflections...personal application... personal prayer points...

On the Offensive

Did you know that the sword of the Spirit mentioned in Ephesians 6 is not only for deflecting a blow from the enemy but also for inflicting blows? So we use the sword of the Spirit not only to defend ourselves against the enemy's temptations and condemnations but also for attack.

In Acts 8, we find this modeled for us in the life of Philip, who shared the gospel with a traveler from Ethiopia who was searching for God. Philip had been preaching the gospel in Samaria, and people were coming to faith. But then God told him, "Go south." And Philip obeyed, like a good soldier prepared for battle. When he came upon the Ethiopian traveler, he used the sword of the Spirit, the Word of God, to proclaim the gospel of Jesus to this man, because he knew God's Word and was able to use it when the right time came.

Make no mistake about it: there's authority and power in the Word of God. Our own words will fall to the ground, but God's Word sticks. God's Word breaks through.

> We are human, but we don't wage war as humans do. We use **God's** mighty weapons, not worldly weapons, to knock down the **strongholds** of human reasoning and to destroy false arguments.
>
> 2 CORINTHIANS 10:3-4 NLT

We could spend all day trying to defend and explain the Bible with our own words, but I have a better idea: use the sword of the Spirit. That's what Philip did, and it's what we need to do as well.

This is something the devil doesn't want you to know. He doesn't want you to start attacking, because if you stay in defensive mode, then he has more freedom to carry out his plans, and he's in control of where the battle takes place. But if you're attacking, he has to worry about defense.

THE LORD'S INVITATION TO HIS PEOPLE

Preach the word of God. Be prepared,
whether the time is favorable or not.
2 TIMOTHY 4:2 NLT

WITH GOD IN PRAYER

Thank Him for the power of His Word.

MOVE BEYOND A FAILURE TO ATTACK

How can you use God's Word—the sword of the Spirit—as an offensive weapon today?

Your own reflections...personal application... personal prayer points...

A Change
of Direction

One morning in the late 1800s, Alfred Nobel, the inventor of dynamite, was reading the newspaper. He was shocked to find his name listed in the obituary column. It was a mistake, but nonetheless, there it was.

In the obituary, he was negatively remembered as someone who made a fortune through explosives, which at that time were used primarily for warfare. Nobel was distressed to see himself described by the obituary as "the merchant of death."

As a result of reading this mistaken obituary, Nobel decided to change the course of his life. He committed himself to world peace. In his will, he left most of his vast fortune for the establishment of an annual prize for "champions of peace," as well as awards in the fields of chemistry, physics, medicine, and literature.

When the name Alfred Nobel is mentioned today, dynamite is rarely the first thing that comes to mind. Rather, we think of the prizes that bear his name. It's all because Alfred Nobel decided to change the course his life was taking.

Another man, living centuries before, also changed the negative course his life was on. His name was Paul, formerly known as Saul of Tarsus. As a relentless persecutor of the early church, he was determined to stop the spread of Christianity. But after a dramatic conversion on the Damascus Road, Paul devoted the rest of his life to preaching the gospel and building the church. Today, we remember him as a missionary, church planter, and author of most of the New Testament epistles.

> We must all stand before Christ
> to be **judged**. We will each receive
> whatever we deserve for the good or evil
> we have **done** in this earthly body.
>
> 2 CORINTHIANS 5:10 NLT

If you were to read your own obituary today, what do you think people would remember you for? It isn't too late to change your direction.

THE LORD'S INVITATION TO HIS PEOPLE

Rest your hope fully upon the grace that is to be brought to you at the revelation of Jesus Christ.

1 PETER 1:13

WITH GOD IN PRAYER

Thank Him for His grace that can empower you for a life that's fully pleasing to Him.

MOVE BEYOND AN EMPTY LIFE

If you were to die today, what would people most likely remember you for? What would your obituary list as your accomplishments? If this is not what you would want it to be—what changes in your life's direction do you need to make today?

Your own reflections...personal application... personal prayer points...

Simple Obedience

Prior to his conversion, Saul was a leading Pharisee and possibly even a member of the Jewish Sanhedrin. He presided over the death of Stephen, the first martyr of the Christian church. After Saul's encounter with Jesus on the Damascus Road resulted in his conversion, the Christians of that day were at first suspicious of his conversion.

So when God directed a believer in Damascus named Ananias to seek out Saul and pray for him, Ananias was understandably reluctant. But Ananias did what God told him to do. He found Saul in the place where God said he would find him. He prayed that the Lord would restore Saul's sight (he'd been blinded by the light when Jesus spoke to him on the Damascus Road), and the Lord did heal Saul's eyes.

> Go, for Saul is my **chosen**
> instrument to take my message to
> the **Gentiles** and to kings, as
> well as to the people of **Israel.**
> ACTS 9:15 NLT

It's interesting that when God wanted to use someone to minister to Saul, He didn't call an apostle like Peter or John. He called an ordinary man. Ananias didn't write any book of the New Testament, raise a dead person back to life, or give a notable sermon that we know about. But he did, by faith, take under his wing a man who would do all of the above and far more. Ananias discipled the newly converted Saul who, in time, became the legendary apostle Paul and probably the greatest preacher in the history of the church.

Thank God for the Ananiases of the kingdom, those who faithfully work behind the scenes to make such a difference in our lives. They may be unknown to man, but they're loved by God.

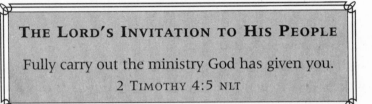

THE LORD'S INVITATION TO HIS PEOPLE

Fully carry out the ministry God has given you.
2 TIMOTHY 4:5 NLT

WITH GOD IN PRAYER

Thank Him for the believers down through history who have been faithful in their service to the Lord.

MOVE BEYOND A LACK OF FAITHFUL OBEDIENCE

What is the specific ministry God has called you to? Are you being faithful in it?

Your own reflections...personal application... personal prayer points...

Characterized by Prayer

God told Ananias to look for Saul—and said he would find Saul praying. Sure enough, that's exactly what Ananias found him doing. I think Saul, in the meantime, probably was asking God to forgive all the wrongs he'd done. Can you imagine how hard it would be to accept God's forgiveness if you not only had been a murderer but also had deliberately hunted down the followers of Jesus Christ and brought about their premature deaths? How hard it would be to have that on your conscience!

But Saul prayed, and in the process discovered that intimacy could be found with this God whom he'd known only in a distant way before.

You can't help but notice, as you read through Paul's epistles, how much prayer characterized his life. So many of his letters begin or end with beautiful prayers. And it was Paul who told us to "pray without ceasing" (1 Thessalonians 5:17).

> The Lord said, "Go over to Straight Street, to the **house** of Judas. When you get there, ask for a man from Tarsus named Saul. He is **praying** to me right now."
> ACTS 9:11 NLT

Paul also practiced what he preached. When he and Silas were thrown into prison for preaching the gospel, they prayed and sang praises to God at midnight, and the other prisoners heard them. Now, who would want to pray at a time like that? But instead of cursing those who put them there, they were blessing God. No wonder the other prisoners were listening to them.

This was the transformation that took place in the life of Paul. He was a man of prayer.

Are you a man or a woman of prayer? Does prayer characterize your life? It should. If you want to live this Christian life effectively, you need to learn how to pray.

THE LORD'S INVITATION TO HIS PEOPLE

Devote yourselves to prayer with
an alert mind and a thankful heart.
COLOSSIANS 4:2 NLT

WITH GOD IN PRAYER

Thank Him for the privilege of actually coming into His presence to present your needs. Thank Him that He hears you when you ask for His help.

MOVE BEYOND PRAYERLESSNESS

What is your own definition of a man or woman of prayer? To be that kind of person, what should your daily time in prayer look like?

Your own reflections...personal application... personal prayer points...

A Word to Dads

A few years ago, someone asked the first President George Bush, "What is your greatest accomplishment in life?" I thought that was an interesting question to ask someone like him, who had quite a long list of achievements.

He could have pointed to a number of political attainments for either him or his children. After all, he was the U.S. ambassador to China, director of the CIA, then vice president for two terms under President Reagan before becoming president himself. Two of his sons became state governors, and, of course, one of them also became president.

Yet here's what George Bush named as his greatest accomplishment: "My children still come home to see me."

There's a man who has his priorities in order.

> He will **turn** the hearts of fathers
> to their children and the **hearts**
> of children to their fathers.
> MALACHI 4:6 ESV

As a pastor, I've visited people who are coming to the end of their lives. I've seen what really matters to them—it always comes back to faith and family. When your life is over, it isn't going to matter how many business deals you made, how many investments you have, or how many things you've accumulated. When it's all said and done, it will come down to the basic values of faith and family.

Tragically, so many men today are abandoning their families, rationalizing that it's because of a midlife crisis, to chase after something they imagine will make them feel younger.

Men, we have to stand by the commitments we've made to our wives and children. We cannot even for a moment consider turning our backs on them.

> ## THE LORD'S INVITATION TO HIS PEOPLE
>
> Fathers, do not provoke your children
> to anger by the way you treat them.
> Rather, bring them up with the discipline
> and instruction that comes from the Lord.
> EPHESIANS 6:4 NLT

WITH GOD IN PRAYER

If you're a husband and father, take time today to pray in detail for your wife and children.

MOVE BEYOND FAILURE IN LEADING YOUR FAMILY

If you're a husband and father, what specific encouragement and guidance does your family need from you now and in the immediate future? What do you need to do now to ensure their future health and well-being, both spiritually and physically?

Your own reflections...personal application... personal prayer points...

Shaped by Suffering

On a recent visit to North Carolina, I drove through a town named Mocksville. I should have been born there. Prior to becoming a Christian, I always loved to mock other people. So when I became a follower of Jesus, I was shocked when I became the one being mocked. People were laughing at me because of my faith in Christ.

This is what happened to Paul, but in a far more intense way. Right after his conversion, he started preaching the gospel in Damascus. He was so powerful and persuasive that the religious leaders wanted him dead.

Their plot was discovered, and Paul's fellow Christians devised a plan to help him escape. They put him in a basket and lowered it over the city wall at night. Think of the irony! Just a short time before, he was Saul of Tarsus, the notorious persecutor of Christians. The hunter had become the hunted. He was getting a taste of his own medicine.

> I take pleasure in my weaknesses, and in the insults, **hardships**, persecutions, and troubles that I suffer for Christ. For when I am **weak**, then I am strong.
>
> 2 CORINTHIANS 12:10 NLT

His name change from Saul to Paul offers insight into the real transformation that took place. The first king of Israel was named Saul. In contrast, the name Paul means "little." It would be like deliberately changing your name from Spike to Squirt. Obviously, God had changed Paul into a man of humility.

Sometimes we want God to take certain things out of our lives that cause us pain. We pray over and over for those things to be removed. But do we ever stop to think how God is using those things in our lives to transform us and make us more like Him?

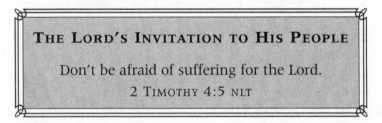

THE LORD'S INVITATION TO HIS PEOPLE

Don't be afraid of suffering for the Lord.
2 TIMOTHY 4:5 NLT

WITH GOD IN PRAYER

Thank Him for the suffering He allows into your life, for your good. And thank Him in advance for the suffering He'll allow in your life in the future.

MOVE BEYOND RESISTANCE TO SUFFERING

How has God used suffering in your life to transform you and make you more like Him? How is He doing this now?

Your own reflections...personal application... personal prayer points...

Destined
for Greatness

It has been said that it takes a steady hand to hold a full cup.

God was planning to give a full cup to the apostle Paul. So He first led Paul into obscurity in the desert of Arabia for a time (see Galatians 1:17). We aren't told what happened there, but we can only presume that Paul drew closer to the Lord in fellowship and communion. It was there that he refined his theology, as evidenced in the New Testament epistles that God later inspired him to write.

This was typical of how God dealt with many people as He prepared them for greater ministry assignments. Joseph was used greatly in the house of Potiphar, but then he was sent to prison for two long years. Moses had forty years of training in the wilderness of Midian before leading the children of Israel out of Egypt. David was anointed king of Israel as a teenager, but it wasn't until he reached the age of thirty that he actually ascended the throne. When Elijah obediently delivered God's message to King Ahab and Queen Jezebel in their court, he was led away to the Brook Cherith for a long while to wait on God.

God was preparing all these men for what lay ahead, just as He did later for Paul.

As you endure this **divine** discipline, remember that God is treating you as his own children. Who ever heard of a child who is never **disciplined** by its father?

HEBREWS 12:7 NLT

When you've gone through the desert of hardship, God will use you to more effectively minister to others. Do you find yourself in a "desert experience"? Maybe God has some training in mind for you.

Remember, you can never be too small for God to use; only too big.

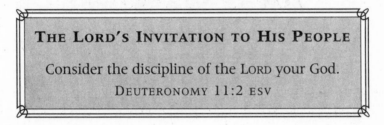

THE LORD'S INVITATION TO HIS PEOPLE

Consider the discipline of the LORD your God.
DEUTERONOMY 11:2 ESV

WITH GOD IN PRAYER

Commit yourself to whatever training and preparation God wants to take you through, whatever this means.

MOVE BEYOND A FEAR OF HARDSHIP

When you think about the kinds of trials and hardships God has taken you through, what purpose do you see in them? In what ways do you think He is trying to change you and refine your character?

Your own reflections...personal application... personal prayer points...

Finishing What We Start

Imagine, for a moment, that you and I are competing in a race of ten laps. When the starter pistol is fired, we take off, and I leave you in my dust. I'm running really fast; you're running really slow.

As I come to the tenth and final lap. I tell myself, *I'm creaming the competition. Before I finish, I'm going to go out and get a Krispy Kreme doughnut.* So I wander off the track.

Ten minutes later, you finally cross the finish line. But I haven't yet returned from my doughnut break.

It's clear I'm a better runner than you. But if I didn't do the tenth lap and cross the finish line, then I've lost the race. It doesn't matter if I led for nine out of ten laps. I had to finish the race I began.

> I will be proud that I did
> not **run** the race in vain.
> PHILIPPIANS 2:16 NLT

In the same way, there are many people who started off with a great burst of energy as they began to follow the Lord. Maybe you're one of them. If so, that's great. But listen: that was then, and this is now. How you were running a year ago, or even a month ago, is no longer significant. But how you're running right now is.

Are you keeping up the pace? Are you persevering? Are you going to make it across the finish line? You can make it if you persevere.

As you live the Christian life, there'll be times when it's hard. You'll have to hold on to God's Word…and to His promise that He'll complete the work He has begun in your life (see Philippians 1:6).

But will you make the effort to cross the finish line?

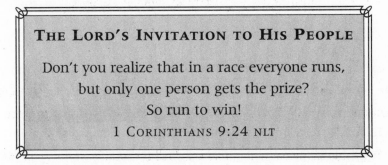

THE LORD'S INVITATION TO HIS PEOPLE

Don't you realize that in a race everyone runs,
but only one person gets the prize?
So run to win!
1 CORINTHIANS 9:24 NLT

WITH GOD IN PRAYER

Ask God to strengthen your endurance in every way—spiritually, physically, emotionally, and mentally.

MOVE BEYOND A LACK OF PERSEVERANCE

How are you running the race of the Christian life right now? Are you persevering? Are you confident that you'll reach the finish line?

Your own reflections...personal application... personal prayer points...

A Wing or a Weight?

I heard about a great concert violinist who was asked about the secret to her great performances. She answered, "Planned neglect. Anything that would keep me from practicing and playing well must be neglected."

I think some of us could use some planned neglect in our lives, because there's a lot more junk in them than we may realize. If you don't believe me, try moving from one house to another. Isn't it amazing how much junk you've collected? The same is true in our lives. We take on things we don't need. Periodically, we needed to jettison this excess weight.

> You were running a good **race**.
> Who cut in on you and kept you
> from **obeying** the truth?
> GALATIANS 5:7 NIV

When the race of life gets difficult, we like to blame circumstances, other people, or sometimes even God. But we need to remember that if we stumble or fall, it's our own fault. The Bible declares, "By his divine power, God has given us everything we need for living a godly life" (2 Peter 1:3 NLT).

The Bible also tells us to "strip off every weight that slows us down, especially the sin that so easily trips us up" (Hebrews 12:1 NLT). Notice the distinction: we're to lay aside not only sin but also the weights that hinder our progress.

In fact, I would suggest periodically asking yourself this question about the uncertain areas of your life: Is it a wing or is it a weight? In other words, does it speed you on your way in this race you're running? Or is it a weight—something that slows you down?

> ## The Lord's Invitation to His People
>
> Let us strip off every weight that
> slows us down, especially the sin that so
> easily trips us up. And let us run with
> endurance the race God has set before us.
> HEBREWS 12:1 NLT

With God in Prayer

Ask Him to give you clarity in understanding and evaluating everything that consumes your time and energy.

Move Beyond Hindrances to Spiritual Progress

Think about your time commitments, responsibilities, activities, and diversions. Are any of these things hindering your spiritual life—slowing you down? What changes do you need to make?

Your own reflections...personal application... personal prayer points...

In Focus

When I was in high school, I went out for track and field. I was a fairly decent short-distance runner, but I was horrible at long distance. I hated to practice. But if ever I saw a pretty girl in the grandstands, I had new motivation for running.

As we run this race of life, we have a better motivation than I had in high school. We run for an audience of one: Jesus Christ. He's watching us. He's praying for us. In fact, the Bible tells us that He "lives forever to intercede with God" on our behalf (Hebrews 7:25 NLT).

This is what gave young Stephen courage when he stood before his accusers who were ready to put him to death. Full of the Holy Spirit, he was given a glimpse of Jesus in heaven and said, "Look, I see the heavens opened and the Son of Man standing in the place of honor at God's right hand!" (Acts 7:56 NLT). Seeing Jesus gave Stephen the ability to run the race and finish it.

Seeing Jesus also gave Simon Peter the ability to walk on water. As he kept the Lord in sight, He did the impossible.

> I will **look** to the LORD.
> MICAH 7:7

Keeping our eyes on Jesus is so important. Why? Because circumstances will disappoint us and at times devastate us. People will let us down and fall short of our expectations. Feelings will come and go. But Jesus will always be there to cheer us on.

He has run before you. He's the ultimate winner. He'll show you how to run. But you have to keep looking to Him.

> ### The Lord's Invitation to His People
>
> Let us fix our eyes on Jesus,
> the author and perfecter of our faith.
> Hebrews 12:2 NIV

With God in Prayer

Take time today to worship your Lord and Savior, Jesus Christ, and to think about the perfection of all He is.

Move Beyond the Wrong Focus

How can you more effectively keep your eyes on Jesus throughout each day?

Your own reflections...personal application... personal prayer points...

The Real Competition

In running competitions, each athlete is assigned to a lane on the track. Each is expected to stay in his assigned lane. In the same way, as you and I run the race of life, our competition isn't with other believers. Rather, our competition is with our enemies—the world, the flesh, and the devil. The goal isn't to outrun other believers; the goal is to outrun those wicked influences that could bring us down.

Maybe your progress in spiritual maturity is not what it should be. You might justify your slow pace by pointing to other people still running behind you. True. But there are probably plenty of people ahead of you too.

However, you're not to concern yourself with who's behind you or who's ahead of you. You're to run the race laid out for you. God hasn't called you to run someone else's race. We're each called to run our own race.

> I run with **purpose** in every step.
> 1 CORINTHIANS 9:26 NLT

An incident from the life of Peter illustrates this truth. After Peter had been restored to the Lord following his denial, Jesus told Peter how his life would end and then said to him, "Follow me." As they were talking, Peter noticed "the disciple Jesus loved" walking behind them. Peter asked, "What about him, Lord?"

Jesus answered, "If I want him to remain alive until I return, what is that to you? As for you, follow me" (John 21:22 NLT). A loose paraphrase would be, "Peter, it's none of your business. Just do what I've told you to do."

Are you keeping your focus on what you know God has called you to do? Are you running as well as you can in the unique race you've been called to finish? Or are you getting distracted by what He's doing in other believers' lives?

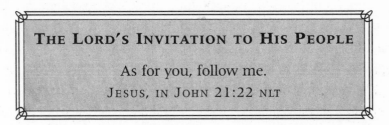

THE LORD'S INVITATION TO HIS PEOPLE

As for you, follow me.
JESUS, IN JOHN 21:22 NLT

WITH GOD IN PRAYER

Thank God for the unique race He has called you to run. Thank Him for how He uniquely created you for this race, for how His grace in Christ Jesus uniquely equips you for running it.

MOVE BEYOND COMPETITION
WITH OTHER BELIEVERS

Are you wholeheartedly pursuing the unique course God has laid out for you? In what ways are you being distracted by what's going on in other believers' lives?

Your own reflections...personal application...
   personal prayer points...

Running to Win

Not long ago, I celebrated my fiftieth birthday. Getting older isn't a depressing thought, because from the day I gave my life to Jesus Christ, life has been an adventure. I don't regret a single day of my life that I've spent following and serving the Lord.

Sure, my life has had some surprises. I've seen people I never thought would make it in the Christian life succeed, and I've seen people fall whom I never thought would fall. Some believers get off to a powerful start, then crash and burn. Others have a rather weak start, then somehow pull it together over time.

Best of all, there are some who start and finish the race with flying colors. I want to be one of those people. Don't you?

> I press on to **reach** the end of the race
> and receive the heavenly **prize** for which
> God, through Christ Jesus, is calling us.
> PHILIPPIANS 3:14 NLT

Here's what we need to remember: we determine how the race we run will turn out. Let me put it another way: if you want to be a winner in the race of life, you can be; if you want to be a loser, you can be. It really comes down to the choices you make on a daily basis.

I've often said that people fall away from the Lord because, for all practical purposes, they choose to. They neglect certain things they should hold on to, and at the same time, allow other things into their lives that they should ignore.

As we make our decisions, our decisions will make us. Make the right decisions today to ensure you'll be running well in the Christian race five and ten and twenty years from now.

I ask you today: Are you offering only a halfhearted effort? Or are you running to win?

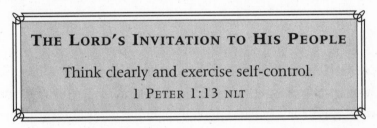

THE LORD'S INVITATION TO HIS PEOPLE

Think clearly and exercise self-control.
1 PETER 1:13 NLT

WITH GOD IN PRAYER

Offer thanks to Him for fully equipping you to win the race He's called you to run.

MOVE BEYOND HALFHEARTEDNESS

What practical steps can you take today to ensure you'll be running well in the Christian race five and ten and twenty years from now?

Your own reflections...personal application... personal prayer points...

Strength in Numbers

Jesus said, "If two of you agree on earth concerning anything that they ask, it will be done for them by My Father in heaven. For where two or three are gathered together in My name, I am there in the midst of them" (Matthew 18:19–20). No question about it: when Christians get together and pray, things happen.

It's good to join forces with other believers. But let's not misunderstand. This verse doesn't mean that if two Christians agree to pray together for a private jet that God will give them one in answer to their prayers. What Jesus was saying is that if two people get their wills in alignment with the will of God, agree together in that area, and keep praying about it, then they'll see results.

> All the believers **devoted** themselves to the apostles' teaching, and to **fellowship**, and to sharing in meals (including the Lord's Supper), and to prayer.
>
> ACTS 2:42 NLT

That's why we need to pray with our Christian friends. That's why we need to call up people and say, "Let's pray about this together." That's why Christians need to be involved in church. If you want to grow spiritually, you must be a part of a congregation of believers. It isn't optional. You need to become part of a group of believers, build friendships with them, and become a productive part of that body. If you aren't involved in a church on a regular basis, I would venture to say you're probably floundering spiritually.

Just as you must eat and drink and breathe to live, you must read the Bible, you must pray, and you must be involved in a church to spiritually live. You'll never outgrow these things. You'll need them until your final day on this earth. And if you neglect these things, I guarantee you'll have a spiritual breakdown.

THE LORD'S INVITATION TO HIS PEOPLE

Let us not neglect our meeting together, as some people do, but encourage one another, especially now that the day of his return is drawing near.
HEBREWS 10:25 NLT

WITH GOD IN PRAYER

Thank Him for all His grace that comes your way through the lives and ministries of other believers.

MOVE BEYOND DISCONNECTION
WITH OTHER BELIEVERS

Are you fully committed to your local church? Are you a productive part of it? Are you actively pursuing ministry and fellowship with others through your church?

Your own reflections...personal application... personal prayer points...

Impeded Prayers

One great hindrance to having our prayers answered is unforgiveness in our hearts. If you harbor bitterness and hatred toward someone else, it can hinder your prayers. So Jesus says that if you're praying and "you have anything against anyone," there's one thing you must do: "forgive him" (Mark 11:25).

Maybe you're thinking, "Wait a second! That person ripped me off. He took advantage of me." But that kind of attitude hinders our prayers. So resolve those things. Work them out. Forgive.

Another thing that can hinder your prayers is having an idol in your heart. In the book of Ezekiel, God warns about those who "set up idols in their hearts" and who "embraced things that will make them fall into sin." Then He says, "Why should I listen to their requests?" (Ezekiel 14:3 NLT). An idol is anything or anyone that takes the place of God in your life. It can be an image you bow down to, but it also can be your career. It can be possessions. It can be your body. It can be anything that's more important to you than God Himself. And it will hinder your prayers.

Who may climb the **mountain** of the LORD?
Who may stand in his holy place? Only those
whose hands and hearts are pure, who do not
worship idols and never tell lies. They
will receive the LORD's blessing and have a
right **relationship** with God their savior.
Such people may seek you and worship in
your **presence**, O God of Jacob.
PSALM 24:3-6 NLT

Unconfessed sin will also bring your prayer life to a screeching halt, as the writer of Psalm 66 affirmed: "If I had not confessed the sin in my heart, the Lord would not have listened" (Psalm 66:18 NLT). As the old saying goes, "If you feel far from God, guess who moved?"

Have you allowed something to get in the way of your relationship with Him? You can change that today.

> ## THE LORD'S INVITATION TO HIS PEOPLE
>
> Come close to God, and God will
> come close to you. Wash your hands,
> you sinners; purify your hearts, for your loyalty
> is divided between God and the world.
>
> JAMES 4:8 NLT

WITH GOD IN PRAYER

Thank Him for making clear in His Word the things that can hinder our communication with Him.

MOVE BEYOND HINDRANCES TO PRAYER

Have you allowed anything to hinder your communication with God in prayer? If so, remove those obstacles now.

Your own reflections...personal application... personal prayer points...

Time with the Father

During a visit to Israel, I had the opportunity to see a replica of a home from the time of Christ. I was surprised to see how sophisticated this home was. It had different rooms, one of which even had a bathtub. It was rather nice. Not all homes in Jesus's day were that way, of course, but some were.

However, Jesus probably didn't live in a home like that, because in Matthew 8:20, He said, "Foxes have holes and birds of the air have nests, but the Son of Man has nowhere to lay His head." The gospel of John offers additional insight: "And everyone went to his own house. But Jesus went to the Mount of Olives" (7:53–8:1).

In this particular passage we don't read that Jesus's disciples were with Him. While everyone else went to their comfortable homes, Jesus went to sleep outside in the open air. He also went to commune with His Father.

> He Himself often **withdrew** into
> the wilderness and prayed.
> LUKE 5:16

While the Pharisees were busy thinking up the newest way to set a trap for Jesus, He was spending time in the presence of His Father. While His enemies were communing with hell, Jesus was communing with heaven. In doing this, He left us an example to follow.

There are times when we need to get away from the crowd and spend time in communion with our heavenly Father. While we don't necessarily need to abandon our homes, we may need to abandon some activities or pursuits.

There are times when we need to get away from the busyness and pressures of life to spend time with the Lord. I can guarantee it will be time well spent.

> ## THE LORD'S INVITATION TO HIS PEOPLE
>
> When you pray, go into your room
> and shut the door and pray to your Father
> who is in secret. And your Father who
> sees in secret will reward you.
> JESUS, IN MATTHEW 6:6 ESV

WITH GOD IN PRAYER

Remember to thank Him often for the privilege of coming into His presence.

MOVE BEYOND PRESSURES
THAT KEEP YOU FROM PRAYER

Make your plans now for getting away from life's routine pressures so you can spend a lengthy amount of concentrated, uninterrupted time with the Lord.

Your own reflections...personal application... personal prayer points...

Poor in Spirit

When Jesus said, "Blessed are the poor in spirit," that word *poor* carries the image of someone shrinking, cowering, cringing. It describes a destitute person, someone completely dependent on others for help.

> Blessed are the poor in spirit,
> for theirs is the **kingdom** of heaven.
> JESUS, IN MATTHEW 5:3

But Jesus wasn't addressing a person's economic situation. Rather, He was dealing with a person's spiritual condition. Let's not miss what He's saying. Blessed, or happy, is the person who recognizes his or her spiritual poverty apart from God. Happy are those who see themselves as they really are in God's sight—lost, hopeless, and helpless.

Apart from Jesus Christ, everyone is spiritually poor. Regardless of our education, accomplishments, or religious knowledge, we're all spiritually destitute.

We may look at someone in prison or the down-and-outer or the drug addict and think, *Now there's someone who's spiritually destitute.* Then we look at ourselves. Maybe we've lived a relatively refined life. Maybe we've had a good education and have accomplished certain things. We say, "I'm not as destitute as that person." In one sense, that may be true. But in another sense, it isn't true at all. Before God, all people are spiritually destitute and unable to help themselves.

Some people have a hard time admitting this. It's hard for us to acknowledge how much we need to reach out to God, how much we need His forgiveness. But if we want to be forgiven, if we want to be happy, then we must humble ourselves and admit our need.

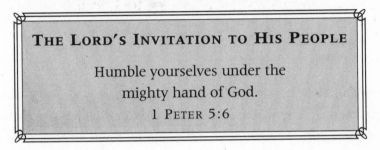

THE LORD'S INVITATION TO HIS PEOPLE

Humble yourselves under the
mighty hand of God.
1 PETER 5:6

WITH GOD IN PRAYER
Acknowledge before Him your true spiritual poverty.

MOVE BEYOND SPIRITUAL PRIDE
AND COMPLACENCY
Do you have a hard time admitting that you're spiritually destitute? If so, humbly confess your pride before God.

Your own reflections...personal application... personal prayer points...

Happy Are the Unhappy

After assessing his spiritual condition on one occasion, the apostle Paul said, "O wretched man that I am! Who will deliver me from this body of death?" (Romans 7:24). Paul saw himself for who he really was—someone in need of help, in need of change. Paul saw his true condition in the light of God's truth and realized he was spiritually destitute and in desperate need. It caused him to be sorry. It caused him to mourn over his being a sinner.

> Blessed are those who **mourn**,
> for they shall be comforted.
> JESUS, IN MATTHEW 5:4

Jesus's statement, "Blessed are those who mourn," could be rephrased as, "Happy are the unhappy." That sounds like a contradiction. How can I be happy if I'm unhappy? But according to the Bible, before you can be truly happy, you have to first be unhappy. Why? Because "godly sorrow produces repentance" (2 Corinthians 7:10).

If you're really sorry for your sin, you'll not only be sad and sorry about it, you'll also do something about it. Specifically, you'll repent of that sin and turn from it.

The Bible says, "Blessed are those whose lawless deeds are forgiven, and whose sins are covered. Blessed is the man to whom the LORD shall not impute sin" (Romans 4:7–8). When we see our spiritual condition and our need for God, we realize there is just one way to become happy—reach out to God and ask for His forgiveness. Then we'll be comforted, because we've come to Jesus Christ.

Although this happiness comes through pain initially, it ultimately brings the greatest happiness of all. Thus, our sorrow leads to joy. But without that sorrow, there would be no joy.

So you see...happy are the unhappy.

THE LORD'S INVITATION TO HIS PEOPLE

Let there be tears for what you have done.
Let there be sorrow and deep grief.
Let there be sadness instead of laughter,
and gloom instead of joy.

JAMES 4:9 NLT

WITH GOD IN PRAYER

Let Him know that you are sorry for the way your sins have grieved Him and for how your sins required the sacrifice of His Son.

MOVE BEYOND SPIRITUAL SORROW

If you're now experiencing sadness and sorrow for a sin—what do you need to do to repent and turn from it?

Your own reflections...personal application... personal prayer points...

Power Under Constraint

What does it mean to be meek? It doesn't imply weakness. Jesus didn't say, "Happy are the weak." He said, "Happy are the meek."

A good definition of meekness is "power under constraint" or "strength under control." The origin of this word's meaning includes a word used to describe the breaking of a powerful stallion. A stallion hasn't lost its will or strength when it has been broken. But the horse has, in essence, surrendered its will to its rider.

What a contradiction of this world's kind of thinking, which says that if you want to get ahead, you must assert yourself. You must stand up for your rights and look out for number one.

> Blessed are the **meek**, for
> they shall inherit the earth.
> JESUS, IN MATTHEW 5:5

Meekness means surrendering your will, your desires, and your ambitions to God. It doesn't mean you have no will, desires, or ambitions. But it does mean you've handed all this over to God. You tell Him, "Lord, I want to channel the energy You've given me for Your glory. I want to be useful to You. I want to make a difference in this world for You, not for me. I'm not looking out for me anymore; I'm looking out for You."

Then, as you begin thinking more about God and less about yourself, you discover you're happy. But it wasn't a result of seeking happiness; it was a result of forgetting about yourself.

In His only autobiographical description of His personality, Jesus said, "I am gentle and lowly in heart" (Matthew 11:29). That's how we should be too. "Let this mind be in you which was also in Christ Jesus" (Philippians 2:5). When we follow His example, our priorities change. A new spiritual quality is produced in us—meekness.

> ## THE LORD'S INVITATION TO HIS PEOPLE
>
> As the elect of God, holy and beloved,
> put on…meekness.
> COLOSSIANS 3:12

WITH GOD IN PRAYER

Make that commitment before Him: "Lord, I want to channel the energy You've given me for Your glory. I want to be useful to You. I want to make a difference in this world for You, not for me. I'm not looking out for me anymore; I'm looking out for You."

MOVE BEYOND SELF-ASSERTIVENESS

What aspects of your will, desires, or ambitions are you selfishly holding on to? When you identify them, surrender these into the Lord's hands.

Your own reflections...personal application... personal prayer points...

Hungry for God

Have you ever been really hungry? My wife has told me, "Everything with you is always extreme. When you're hungry, you always say, 'I'm starving to death.' Can't you just be sort of hungry?" But that's how it happens. I won't feel hungry, but then all of a sudden, it hits me: I'm ready to eat. My wife's hunger, on the other hand, is the kind that builds up more slowly.

> Blessed are those who **hunger** and **thirst**
> for righteousness, for they shall be filled.
> JESUS, IN MATTHEW 5:6

If you've ever been really hungry or thirsty, you have an idea of what Jesus was speaking of in Matthew 5:6. It's a picture of someone who's hungry and thirsty for God Himself, someone who hungers and thirsts for righteousness. This is a person who's fed up with sin and self-pursuit and who craves God— a person who wants God more than anything else. The psalmist said, "As the deer pants for the water brooks, so pants my soul for You, O God" (Psalm 42:1). This should be our attitude as well.

Are you hungry for God? Do you really want to know Him? Do you crave a holy life? Do you hunger for God's best for you? That's the attitude we need if we want to be truly happy people. We need to hunger for the things of God.

If you want to be happy, live a holy life. Happiness will come from pursuing holiness and righteousness and godliness. What a wise pursuit that is! No man or woman will ever look back on such a life that's dedicated to God and say, "I really wasted my life."

So put yourself in the way of righteousness. Put yourself in the way of God.

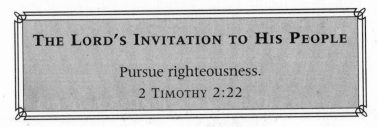

THE LORD'S INVITATION TO HIS PEOPLE

Pursue righteousness.
2 TIMOTHY 2:22

WITH GOD IN PRAYER

Talk with Him about your hunger for righteousness.

MOVE BEYOND A LACK OF SPIRITUAL HUNGER

What really is the righteousness you hunger for? What does it look like? How has God helped you to understand it?

Your own reflections...personal application...
personal prayer points...

Being Merciful

In Matthew 5, Jesus's "Blessed are…" statements, known as the Beatitudes, are not given haphazardly. There's a sequence, an intentional order to them.

First we see ourselves as we are—poor in spirit. Then we mourn over this and repent (verse 4). Then we assess our condition and become truly meek (verse 5). Then, as we're emptied of ourselves, we find a great hunger for God Himself (verse 6).

This leads to the next step—becoming people of mercy who understand and sympathize with others—including those who don't yet know God, who are outside of His forgiveness, and who are without His help.

> Blessed are the **merciful**,
> for they shall obtain mercy.
> Jesus, in Matthew 5:7

A good litmus test to determine whether you've gone through the earlier steps and reached this one is your attitude toward others who have sinned. When another Christian has fallen into sin, what's your attitude? Do you think, *What an idiot! I would never do that?*

And when you see someone who's without Christ, do you say to yourself, *What a fool. I don't know how anyone could live that way?*

If that's your attitude, then you aren't merciful.

How much do you know of God's forgiveness? Do you remember you were once in the same place? God has graciously reached out to us and forgiven us; we, of all people, should be merciful toward others.

Those who look down on others show that they know little about God's mercy and grace. The more righteous a person is, the more merciful he or she will be. The more sinful a person is, the more harsh and critical he or she will be.

"Blessed are the merciful." May God help us to be merciful—to see people as He sees them.

> ## THE LORD'S INVITATION TO HIS PEOPLE
>
> Be merciful, just as your Father also is merciful.
> JESUS, IN LUKE 6:36

WITH GOD IN PRAYER

Think about the endless mercy He has shown to you and offer Him your thanksgiving, praise, and worship.

MOVE BEYOND A LACK OF MERCY

Who do you need to extend mercy to today?

Your own reflections...personal application... personal prayer points...

Ready to Go?

If the rapture happened today, would you be ready to go?

The Bible says Christ is coming for those who are watching and waiting for Him. Does the thought that Jesus could come back today make your heart leap? Or does it make your heart sink?

Any person who's right with God should be excited about the imminent return of Jesus. Your attitude says much about where you are spiritually. If the thought of His return brings joy to your heart, that would be an indication you're walking with God. But if it causes fear, it's an indication that something isn't right spiritually.

> We should live in this evil world with wisdom, righteousness, and **devotion** to God, while we **look** forward with hope to that wonderful day when the **glory** of our great God and Savior, Jesus Christ, will be **revealed**.
> TITUS 2:12–13 NLT

As Jesus spoke to His disciples about the end times, He closed His teaching with a personal exhortation: "Take heed to yourselves, lest your hearts be weighed down with carousing, drunkenness, and cares of this life, and that Day come on you unexpectedly. For it will come as a snare on all those who dwell on the face of the whole earth" (Luke 21:34–35).

As followers of Christ, we need to be living in such a way that we're ready for His return. We need to be living in such a way that every moment counts. One day, each of us will be held accountable for how we spent our time, our resources, and our lives. Let's not waste them. Let's allow the anticipation of the Lord's imminent return to keep us on our toes spiritually. Let's allow it to motivate us to live godly lives.

THE LORD'S INVITATION TO HIS PEOPLE

So you, too, must keep watch! For you do not know the day or hour of my return.

JESUS, IN MATTHEW 25:13 NLT

WITH GOD IN PRAYER

Thank Him for the promise in His Word that Jesus will return.

MOVE BEYOND UNREADINESS FOR CHRIST'S RETURN

What thoughts and emotions do you experience as you honestly face the fact that Jesus could return to earth before you finish reading this page?

Your own reflections...personal application... personal prayer points...

Wanted: Disciples

John Wesley, the great English evangelist, once said, "Give me a hundred men who fear nothing but sin and desire nothing but God, and I do not care if they be clergymen or laymen. Such men alone will shake the gates of hell and set up the kingdom of heaven on earth."

I don't know if Wesley ever found such men. But I know Jesus did.

Jesus called these men to be His disciples. In the book of Acts, they were described as "these who have turned the world upside down" (Acts 17:6). The people who called them that didn't mean it as a compliment. But their description acknowledged the amazing impact the disciples were having.

If there was ever a time in history when the world needed to be turned upside down—or should I say right side up—that time is now. But if it's going to happen, it will need to be through committed believers like the ones John Wesley was looking for—people who fear nothing but sin and desire nothing but God. No fair-weather followers need apply. God is looking for disciples.

> Jesus said to His disciples, "If anyone **desires** to come after Me, let him deny himself, and take up his cross, and **follow** Me."
>
> MATTHEW 16:24

So what does it mean to be a disciple? It simply means you take your plans, your goals, and your aspirations and place them at the feet of Jesus. It simply means saying, "Not my will, but Yours be done."

Let's commit ourselves to being true disciples of Jesus Christ. Not mere fair-weather followers, but disciples.

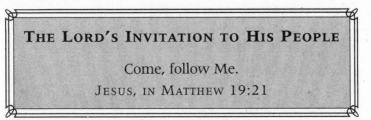

THE LORD'S INVITATION TO HIS PEOPLE

Come, follow Me.

JESUS, IN MATTHEW 19:21

WITH GOD IN PRAYER

Commit yourself to being a true follower and disciple of Jesus Christ.

MOVE BEYOND LACK OF COMMITMENT IN FOLLOWING CHRIST

What does it truly mean to you to be a disciple of Jesus Christ? Does it mean all that it should mean?

Your own reflections...personal application... personal prayer points...

Saved Soul, Wasted Life

A poll was taken not long ago asking Americans what they thought was their main purpose in life. The responses were interesting. You would think some top answers would be, say, "to make a contribution to society," or, "to have a meaningful life." But most people said the main purpose of life was "enjoyment and personal fulfillment." And it's interesting to note that half of those polled identified themselves as born-again Christians.

According to the Bible, the purpose of life is not enjoyment and personal fulfillment. The Bible teaches that we're put on this earth to bring glory to God. We need to mark that well in our minds and hearts.

Speaking through the prophet Isaiah, God said, "Bring all who claim me as their God, for I have made them for my glory. It was I who created them" (Isaiah 43:7 NLT). We were created to glorify God in all that we do with our lives.

> Fear God and keep his **commandments**,
> for this is the whole duty of man.
> ECCLESIASTES 12:13 ESV

Are you using your resources and talents for His glory? Sometimes we think God has given us this life to do with what we will. We'll say, *Lord, this time is mine. Your time is on Sunday morning; the rest belongs to me,* or, *Here's my plan for my life, Lord; here's what I want to accomplish,* or, *This is my money; here's your 10 percent, Lord; I give a waitress more than that, but 10 percent is all You get.* We develop a false concept of God.

It's possible to have a saved soul and yet live a wasted life.

If you were asked today, "What's the main purpose of life?" what would you say?

THE LORD'S INVITATION TO HIS PEOPLE

Whatever you do, do all to the glory of God.

1 CORINTHIANS 10:31

WITH GOD IN PRAYER

Ask Him to keep you from living a wasted life.

MOVE BEYOND A WASTED LIFE

What is your main purpose in life? Is it the advancement of God's kingdom and His glory? If so, are you truly using your resources and time and talents for His kingdom and glory? If not, what immediate changes do you need to make?

Your own reflections...personal application... personal prayer points...

The Time Is Now

"It was the best of times, it was the worst of times." That's the opening line to Charles Dickens's classic novel *A Tale of Two Cities*. In many ways, you could use the same words to describe our world today.

In 1948, Gen. Omar Bradley made this statement: "We have grasped the mystery of the atom and we have rejected the Sermon on the Mount. The world has achieved brilliance without conscience. Ours is a world of nuclear giants and ethical infants." If that was true in 1948, it's definitely true now.

In many ways, things have never been darker spiritually in our world and in our country. Despite all of the incredible technological advances we've made in recent years, it seems like we have regressed morally.

At the same time, we see rays of hope where God is intervening, where people are coming to faith.

> Now it is high time to **awake** out of sleep; for **now** our salvation is nearer than when we first believed.
> ROMANS 13:11

As we see the direction our world is going, recognize that these are signs of the times, reminders that the Lord is coming back. Jesus told us there would be certain things we should look for to alert us to the fact that His coming is near. Then He added, "When these things begin to happen, look up and lift up your heads, because your redemption draws near" (Luke 21:28).

If ever there was a time to be sure our lives are right with God, if ever there was a time to be certain we're walking with Him so we can gladly look up as our redemption draws near, that time is now.

> ## THE LORD'S INVITATION TO HIS PEOPLE
>
> Be careful how you live. Don't live like fools,
> but like those who are wise.
> EPHESIANS 5:15 NLT

WITH GOD IN PRAYER

Thank Him for the places in this world where many people are coming to faith in Jesus Christ.

MOVE BEYOND UNREADINESS
FOR CHRIST'S RETURN

At this moment, is your life right with God? Make sure that it is. Do whatever it takes to be certain of this.

Your own reflections...personal application... personal prayer points...

Immortality

Historian Will Durant, when he reached the age of seventy, said, "To live forever would be the greatest curse imaginable."

Will we live forever? The answer is yes…and no. Will our bodies live forever? No. Will our bodies cease to exist at one point? Absolutely. But the soul is immortal. Every one of us has a soul. It's the soul that gives each of us uniqueness and personality. That part of us will live forever.

Today, many people are searching after physical immortality, that elusive fountain of youth. Sometimes it's hard for us to accept the fact that life is passing and death is approaching. One day, you'll wake up and realize you have more life behind you than you have in front of you. But the question we should be asking is not, "Can I find immorality?" Rather, it should be, "Where will I spend my immortality?"

If you have put your faith in Jesus Christ and have asked Him to forgive you of your sins, the Bible teaches that when you die you'll go immediately into the presence of God in heaven. That's God's promise to you.

> These dying bodies cannot **inherit** what will last forever. But let me reveal to you a wonderful **secret**. We will not all die, but we will all be **transformed**!
> 1 CORINTHIANS 15:50-51 NLT

But God promises not only life beyond the grave. He also promises life during life—not just an existence, but a life that's worth living. Jesus said, "My purpose is to give them a rich and satisfying life" (John 10:10 NLT).

That's the hope and promise for all Christians. That's why the believer doesn't have to be afraid to die…or afraid to live.

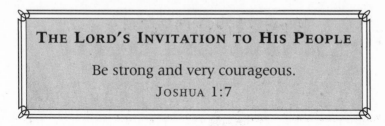

THE LORD'S INVITATION TO HIS PEOPLE

Be strong and very courageous.

JOSHUA 1:7

WITH GOD IN PRAYER

Thank Him for the promises in His Word of eternal life for all who believe in Jesus Christ for salvation.

MOVE BEYOND THE FEAR OF DYING

Are you unafraid to die? And are you unafraid to live your life as a bold witness of Jesus Christ?

Your own reflections...personal application... personal prayer points...

The Truth About the Devil

Martin Luther had it right when he wrote the words of the hymn "A Mighty Fortress Is Our God": "For still our ancient foe doth seek to work us woe; his craft and power are great, and, armed with cruel hate, on earth is not his equal."

If you're a Christian, you need to know you have an adversary out there. He wants to trip you up. He wants to drag you down.

We should never underestimate the devil. He's a sly and skillful adversary. He has had many years of experience dealing with humanity. That's why there are some important things we need to remember about the devil—things the devil doesn't want us to know.

We need to understand that Satan is nowhere near to being the equal of God. God is omnipotent, which means He's all-powerful. God is omniscient, which means He's all-knowing. God is omnipresent, which means He's present everywhere.

> The time for **judging** this world
> has come, when Satan, the ruler
> of this **world**, will be cast out.
> JESUS, IN JOHN 12:31 NLT

In sharp and direct contrast, the devil doesn't reflect any of these divine attributes. Although he's powerful, Satan is not omnipotent. Nor is Satan omniscient; his knowledge is limited. Finally, he's not omnipresent. While

God can be everywhere at the same time, Satan can be in only one place at one time.

Most important of all, we need to know that the devil was soundly defeated at the Cross. There he lost his stranglehold on the life of the human race. As a Christian, you've been set free by the power of Jesus Christ.

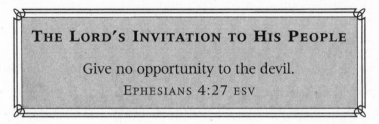

THE LORD'S INVITATION TO HIS PEOPLE

Give no opportunity to the devil.
EPHESIANS 4:27 ESV

WITH GOD IN PRAYER

Give thanks that in His death and resurrection, Jesus Christ has defeated the devil forever.

MOVE BEYOND IGNORANCE ABOUT THE DEVIL

In the spiritual warfare that we face in the Christian life, are you as knowledgeable as you need to be about your enemy?

Your own reflections...personal application... personal prayer points...

A Time Like This

The Old Testament book of Esther is a wonderful love story—a story of what God did in the life of a woman to literally save a nation. Esther was a Jew who was plucked out of obscurity through an unusual chain of events and was made queen to Xerxes, king of Persia. Meanwhile, a wicked man named Haman had been devising a plot to put to death the fifteen million Jews in that kingdom. So Mordecai, Esther's uncle, came to the palace, wanting Esther to use her influence to help her people.

He sent word to Esther:

> Do not think in your heart that you will escape in the king's palace any more than all the other Jews. For if you remain completely silent at this time, relief and deliverance will arise for the Jews from another place, but you and your father's house will perish. Yet who knows whether you have come to the kingdom for such a time as this? (Esther 4:13–14)

> Who knows whether you have come to
> the kingdom for **such a time** as this?
> ESTHER 4:14

Wherever you may find yourself today, know that God has put you where you are for such a time as this. He has put you in that job or at that school. He has put you in that neighborhood. There are opportunities to seize. You need to take hold of them.

Yet the dilemma of Esther is similar to that of many believers today. They've been delivered from sin. They've found safety in the church. And they've grown lazy. They have no vision. Of course, the devil is happy with this, because that's exactly how he wants Christians to live. Be a complacent, apathetic Christian, and the devil will be generally pleased.

THE LORD'S INVITATION TO HIS PEOPLE

Never be lazy, but work hard
and serve the Lord enthusiastically.
ROMANS 12:11 NLT

WITH GOD IN PRAYER

Thank Him for the opportunities He is setting before you this very day. Ask Him to make you fully aware of them, and then make the most of them.

MOVE BEYOND COMPLACENCY AND APATHY

What are the opportunities God is setting before you today? What steps do you need to take to ensure that you please Him in how you respond to each one?

Your own reflections...personal application... personal prayer points...

At Every Turn

During the Korean War, a unit known as Baker Company was separated from its regiment, and enemy forces were advancing on them. For several hours, no word came from Baker Company. Finally, radio contact was made, and when asked for a report of its situation, Baker Company replied, "The enemy is to the east of us. The enemy is to the west of us. The enemy is to the south of us. The enemy is to the north of us." Then, after a brief pause, a voice continued, "And this time, we're not going to let them escape."

It seems that way in the life of the believer. The enemy is at every turn. Yet some Christians don't realize that the Christian life is not a playground but a battleground. They're oblivious to the fact that a war is raging. And in this war, they're either winning or losing.

> Lead me, O LORD, in Your **righteousness** because of my enemies; make Your way **straight** before my face.
> PSALM 5:8

In a battle, it's always better to be an aggressor instead of a defender, because the defender is simply waiting for the enemy's next attack, hoping he'll survive. If we, as believers, are always defending, then the devil is in the superior position. But if we're attacking, we are in the superior position.

When the apostle Paul wrote about the armor of God, he mentioned one offensive weapon—"the sword of the Spirit, which is the word of God" (Ephesians 6:17 NLT). Make no mistake about it: there's authority and power in the Word of God. God's Word sticks. God's Word breaks through. God's Word impacts.

When the Enemy has you surrounded, keep him on the defensive with the Word of God.

The Lord's Invitation to His People

Put on salvation as your helmet, and take the sword of the Spirit, which is the word of God.

EPHESIANS 6:17 NLT

WITH GOD IN PRAYER

Thank Him for the power of His Word. Thank Him specifically for what the Bible has meant in your life.

MOVE BEYOND BEING PASSIVE
IN SPIRITUAL WARFARE

Who can you share the Word of God with today as you join in the battle for truth and the gospel?

Your own reflections...personal application... personal prayer points...

What Do You Think?

When Jesus walked this earth, He blew the cover of the religious elite of the day—the Pharisees who smugly thought that if they didn't commit certain sins, they were okay. They somehow had rationalized that immoral thoughts were not in themselves sinful. But Jesus told them this:

> You have heard that it was said to those of old, "You shall not commit adultery." But I say to you that whoever looks at a woman to lust for her has already committed adultery with her in his heart. (Matthew 5:27–28)

They didn't like hearing that a whole lot.

What was Jesus pointing out to these men—and to us as well? He was emphasizing the importance of our minds. Our hearts. Our attitudes. That's because sin is not merely a matter of actions and deeds. It's something within the heart and the mind that leads to the action.

> As [a person] **thinks**
> in his heart, so is he.
> PROVERBS 23:7

Sin deceives you into thinking that if you've contemplated a wrong act but haven't committed it, you're okay. In reality, if you keep thinking about it, it may be only a matter of time until that sinful thought becomes an action. Even if it doesn't, that thought alone is spiritually destructive. So you need to go out of your way as a Christian to protect your thoughts.

Satan recognizes the value of getting a foothold in the realm of your thoughts and imaginations, because he knows this will prepare the way for an evil thought to eventually become an evil action.

Remember the saying: "Sow a thought, reap an act. Sow an act, reap a habit. Sow a habit, reap a character. Sow a character, reap a destiny." It all starts with a thought.

THE LORD'S INVITATION TO HIS PEOPLE

Set your mind on things above,
not on things on the earth.
COLOSSIANS 3:2

WITH GOD IN PRAYER

Ask Him to be actively at work in helping you identify wrong thoughts and in purifying your mind and heart.

MOVE BEYOND SIN'S DECEPTION

Have you been too tolerant of evil thoughts? Do you allow them to linger and hang on in your mind?

Your own reflections...personal application... personal prayer points...

A Place for Jesus

Imagine being at home tonight and getting ready to go to bed, when suddenly you hear someone knocking at your door. You go and open it. Lo and behold, it's Jesus!

How would you react?

Of course, we know this isn't going to happen. The Lord isn't going to come bodily to your home and knock on the front door. But let your imagination run wild for a moment and pretend that He did exactly that. Jesus Himself has been standing at your door and knocking. Will you open wide the door and gladly welcome Him in? Or will you feel a little apprehensive?

> I pray that from his glorious, unlimited resources he will **empower** you with inner strength through his Spirit. Then Christ will make his **home** in your hearts as you trust in him. Your roots will **grow** down into God's love and keep you strong.
>
> EPHESIANS 3:16–17 NLT

The fact is, we should be living our lives in such a way that Jesus Christ Himself could come walking into our homes at any moment and we would welcome Him without embarrassment.

The Bible says Christ should be able to settle down and be at home in our hearts. That's the picture Paul gave to the church of Ephesus, as he mentioned his concern for them. In effect he said, "I pray that Christ will be more and more at home in your hearts." This doesn't just refer to Christ being present in their hearts; the reality is that He already lives in the heart of every believer. The point Paul made was that Christ should feel at home in their hearts.

Does Jesus feel at home in your heart right now? Is He comfortable there? Is He at ease?

THE LORD'S INVITATION TO HIS PEOPLE

Love the LORD your God with all your heart.
DEUTERONOMY 6:5

WITH GOD IN PRAYER

Ask the Lord Jesus to show you any attitude or thought in your heart that is unpleasant or offensive to Him. Let Him know how much you want Him to feel at home in your heart.

MOVE BEYOND A HEART WHERE CHRIST ISN'T AT HOME

Identify the wrong thoughts and attitudes that need to be cleaned out of your heart. Confess these things and repent of them. Ask for the Lord's enablement in doing this and doing it completely.

Your own reflections...personal application... personal prayer points...

A Time to Sit

When the Lord walked this earth, He had no place to call home (see Matthew 8:20). But there was something He liked about a home in Bethany where a man named Lazarus lived with his two sisters, Mary and Martha. Perhaps Martha was a great cook. Maybe they were wonderful hosts.

Mary and Martha were quite different from each other. Mary was the quiet, contemplative type. Martha was the assertive, grab-the-bull-by-the-horns type.

One day, Jesus came to their home. Martha thought it would be a good idea to make Him a meal. She went into the kitchen and started working. Meanwhile, Mary thought it would be a great opportunity to sit at Jesus's feet and hear what He had to say.

> Surely it is you who love the people;
> all the **holy ones** are in your hand.
> At your feet they all bow down, and
> from you **receive** instruction.
> DEUTERONOMY 33:3 NIV

As Mary was sitting there, taking it all in, Martha was working frantically in the kitchen—she "was distracted with much serving" (Luke 10:40). And she was growing frustrated because Mary wasn't helping her.

Finally she could contain herself no longer. Coming out of the kitchen, she looked down at Mary and Jesus and said, "Lord, do You not care that my sister has left me to serve alone? Therefore tell her to help me" (verse 40).

Jesus responded, "Martha, Martha, you are worried and troubled about many things. But one thing is needed, and Mary has chosen that good part, which will not be taken away from her" (verses 41–42).

Sometimes we do the same thing as Martha. We get so worked up. Like Martha, we sometimes offer activity instead of adoration, work instead of worship, and perspiration instead of inspiration. There's a time to sit, and there's a time to move.

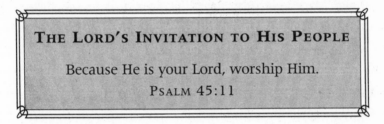

THE LORD'S INVITATION TO HIS PEOPLE

Because He is your Lord, worship Him.

PSALM 45:11

WITH GOD IN PRAYER

In this moment, offer your Lord adoration and worship.

MOVE BEYOND ACTIVITY THAT STIFLES WORSHIP

Are you taking enough time to sit at the feet of Jesus each day? If not—what specific changes do you need to make in your schedule?

Your own reflections...personal application... personal prayer points...

In His Time

Martha and Mary were close friends of Jesus, and so was their brother, Lazarus. So, as we read in John 11, when Lazarus became sick, Martha and Mary immediately sent word to Jesus.

It was a serious illness. No doubt they thought the Lord would drop whatever He was doing and make a beeline to Bethany to get Lazarus off his sickbed. So they waited for Him expectantly.

Meanwhile, Mary and Martha were no doubt saying, "Jesus will come. Any moment now, He'll be here."

But He didn't show up on the day they wanted Him to.

And He didn't come the next day or the day after that.

Lazarus had now passed from sickness to death. In their minds, all hope was gone. By the time Jesus arrived in Bethany, Lazarus had been in the tomb for four days. The two sisters did not know that Jesus had intentionally delayed His coming to them.

> Lazarus is **dead.**
> JESUS, IN JOHN 11:14

Martha walked up to Him and said, "Lord, if You had been here, my brother would not have died" (verse 21). Loose paraphrase: "Jesus, You blew it. You had the perfect situation here. You could have healed him, but You didn't show up."

Jesus got immediately to the bigger issue. He told her, "Your brother will rise again" (verse 23).

Martha replied, "I know that he will rise again in the resurrection at the last day" (verse 24).

Jesus said, "I am the resurrection and the life. He who believes in Me, though he may die, he shall live. And whoever lives and believes in Me shall never die. Do you believe this?" (verses 25–26).

Martha still didn't quite get it. That's because she was thinking of what was temporarily good. But Jesus was thinking of what was eternally good.

Mary and Martha would soon learn that Jesus's delay was for their sake. They would discover this lesson in the most wonderful way imaginable.

THE LORD'S INVITATION TO HIS PEOPLE

Trust in the LORD with all your heart,
and lean not on your own understanding.

PROVERBS 3:5

WITH GOD IN PRAYER

Have your heart and mind been limited in what you trust and expect God to do in your life? Confess this to Him.

MOVE BEYOND SPIRITUAL SHORTSIGHTEDNESS

Tell God your true desire to trust and expect His work in your life—now and for eternity.

Your own reflections...personal application... personal prayer points...

When God Seems Late

Sometimes God won't come through as quickly as we want Him to. That's the dilemma that Mary and Martha faced when their brother, Lazarus, died. It was not until four days later that Jesus finally arrived. But this delay was for their good. Here was the problem: Mary and Martha wanted only a healing. But Jesus wanted a resurrection.

Shortly after he arrived in Bethany, Jesus asked for the tomb to be opened. Then He called out to Lazarus…and Mary and Martha's brother walked out of the tomb! Jesus brought Lazarus back to life, and as a result, many believed in Jesus. Mary and Martha's faith was strengthened, as well as that of the disciples.

Lazarus, **come forth**!

JESUS, IN JOHN 11:43

Sometimes we limit God. Sometimes we think God must work on our schedules. But God will not be bound by time. God will not be bound by our schedules. God will work when He chooses and with whom He chooses. Therefore, there will be times when our circumstances don't make sense. Even then, we need to trust Him.

Like Mary and Martha, we often say, *God, if You loved me, You would solve this problem. You would take care of this need.* But God says, *I won't do it at this time, because I love you; I have something better for you.*

God wants to do something greater in your life. Will you let Him?

THE LORD'S INVITATION TO HIS PEOPLE

Call to Me, and I will answer you,
and show you great and mighty things,
which you do not know.

JEREMIAH 33:3

WITH GOD IN PRAYER

For your ministry to others in Jesus's name, ask Him to do something greater in your life than you can possibly imagine.

MOVE BEYOND LIMITING GOD

Are you feeling disappointed with God because of His timing in doing what only He can do? If so, think about what lessons He is wanting you to learn. Talk about this with Him.

Your own reflections...personal application... personal prayer points...

Learning to Yield

I read a story about a communication that took place some time ago between a U.S. naval ship and Canadian authorities off the coast of Newfoundland. The Canadians warned the Americans, "Please divert your course fifteen degrees to the south to avoid a collision."

The Americans responded, "Recommend you divert your course fifteen degrees to the north to avoid a collision."

The Canadians said, "Negative. You'll have to divert your course fifteen degrees to the south to avoid a collision."

The Americans: "This is the captain of a U.S. Navy ship. I say again, divert your course."

"No. I say again, you divert your course."

"This is the aircraft carrier USS *Lincoln,* the second largest ship in the United States Atlantic fleet. We are accompanied by three destroyers, three cruisers, numerous support vessels. I demand that you change your course fifteen degrees north. I say again, change your course fifteen degrees north, or countermeasures will be undertaken to assure the safety of our ship."

After a brief moment of silence, the Canadians responded: "This is a lighthouse. It's your call."

> The wisdom of the **prudent**
> is to understand his way.
> PROVERBS 14:8

Sometimes we don't like what God wants us to do, and we want Him to change course, when, in reality, we should change.

We need to understand that God's plans are better than ours. That doesn't mean they're always the easiest plans for us or even the most appealing at the moment. As we go through life, there will be times when we might not like the plan of God. But in the long run, God's plans for us are always better.

THE LORD'S INVITATION TO HIS PEOPLE

Live...for the will of God.
1 PETER 4:2

WITH GOD IN PRAYER

Ask Him to give you greater clarity in understanding His will for your life in every area.

MOVE BEYOND FAILURE
TO APPRECIATE GOD'S WISDOM

In what area or areas of life do you sense that God is trying to change your course? What steps of change do you need to take?

Your own reflections...personal application... personal prayer points...

Halfhearted Commitment

God told Abraham (who was first called Abram), "Leave your native country, your relatives, and your father's family, and go to the land that I will show you" (Genesis 12:1 NLT).

Abraham obeyed—but not completely. Instead of leaving all his father's family behind, he took along his nephew Lot, the son of his father's brother: "And they departed to go to the land of Canaan. So they came to the land of Canaan" (Genesis 12:5).

When you read about Abraham and his nephew Lot in Genesis, you might think at first glance that both were spiritual men. But a closer examination reveals this wasn't the case.

Abraham lived for God; Lot, on the other hand, lived for himself. Abraham walked in the Spirit; Lot walked in the flesh. Abraham lived by faith; Lot lived by sight. And most significantly, Abraham walked with God, while Lot walked with Abraham.

Unfortunately, because of Lot's halfhearted commitment to the Lord, he would became a drain on Abraham in many ways, including spiritually.

> I find that your actions do not meet the **requirements** of my God.
> JESUS, IN REVELATION 3:2 NLT

Sadly, Abraham's descendants would reap the results of Abraham's imperfect choice for centuries to come. Lot eventually took possession of land that was adjacent to the land where Abraham settled. There Lot became the father of a son named Moab and a son named Ben-Ammi. Their descendants—the Moabites and the Ammonites—would eventually become bitter enemies of Abraham's descendants, the nation of Israel.

Have ungodly influences been wearing you down lately? Has a certain relationship or pursuit become a spiritual drain in your life? Have you been compromising?

If so, make a change. It isn't too late.

THE LORD'S INVITATION TO HIS PEOPLE

Get out! Get out and leave your captivity,
where everything you touch is unclean.
Get out of there and purify yourselves.

ISAIAH 52:11 NLT

WITH GOD IN PRAYER

Ask Him to show you areas where you're cutting corners in your obedience to Him. Express to Him your desire to serve and obey Him wholeheartedly.

MOVE BEYOND HALFHEARTED COMMITMENT

What new action step do you need to take today in faith and wholehearted commitment to the Lord your God?

Your own reflections...personal application... personal prayer points...

Against All Odds

Jehoshaphat, king of Judah, faced a dilemma. His enemies greatly outnumbered him, and they were coming to destroy him. A messenger came and warned Jehoshaphat about the gigantic army headed toward Jerusalem, bent on Judah's destruction.

Their situation was hopeless. There was no way the king could successfully repel this invading force with the forces at hand. His kingdom would be destroyed.

> In the day of my **trouble**
> I sought the Lord.
> PSALM 77:2

What did Jehoshaphat do? The Bible says he "set himself to seek the LORD" (2 Chronicles 20:3). He prayed these words:

O our God.... We are powerless against this great horde that is coming against us. We do not know what to do, but our eyes are on you. (verse 12 ESV)

And God's answer came:

Thus says the LORD to you, "Do not be afraid and do not be dismayed at this great horde, for the battle is not yours but God's.... Stand firm,

hold your position, and see the salvation of the LORD on your behalf."
(verses 15, 17 ESV)

Jehoshaphat and his army went out to meet their enemies, but they put the worship team out front. The Bible says that when they began to sing and praise the Lord, the enemy started fighting among themselves and eventually destroyed one another.

Maybe you're facing what seems an impossible situation right now. You see no way out. But God can see it.

Call on Him. Then stand still and see what He will do.

THE LORD'S INVITATION TO HIS PEOPLE

Call on Me in the day of trouble; I will deliver you, and you shall honor and glorify Me.
PSALM 50:15 AMP

WITH GOD IN PRAYER

Set yourself to seek the Lord. No matter how difficult the circumstances you face, give priority to worshiping Him.

MOVE BEYOND YOUR IMPOSSIBLE SITUATION

Make sure you are fully and consistently seeking God's help, even while you are faithfully carrying out the responsibilities you know are yours.

Your own reflections...personal application... personal prayer points...

Keep Moving!

It's clear we're living in the last days. All around us, the signs that Jesus and the prophets told us to look for are taking place before our very eyes.

The devil and his demons are doing their dirty work, but this shouldn't surprise us. The Bible warns that in the last days things will go from bad to worse.

One of the signs will be apostasy—an abandonment of the faith by some who have called themselves Christians. They'll fall away and follow deceiving spirits and things taught by demons.

Could you or I ever become one of these spiritual casualties? Could you or I ever fall away from the Lord? Without question, the potential and even the propensity for such sin lies within each of us. I have the potential to fall. So do you.

> The Holy Spirit tells us **clearly** that in the last times some will turn away from the true faith; they will follow **deceptive** spirits and teachings that come from **demons**.
>
> 1 TIMOTHY 4:1 NLT

That's why we must give careful attention to Scripture's warnings of likely pitfalls. There are things we must be alert to as we live in the last days. As the apostle Paul wrote,

The night is far spent, the day is at hand. Therefore let us cast off the works of darkness, and let us put on the armor of light. (Romans 13:12)

Your relationship with Jesus Christ needs constant maintenance and cultivation. The day you stop growing spiritually is the day you'll start to become weak and vulnerable to the devil's attacks. The best way to not go backward is to keep moving forward.

THE LORD'S INVITATION TO HIS PEOPLE

Live holy and godly lives as you look
forward to the day of God and speed its coming.
2 PETER 3:11–12 NIV

WITH GOD IN PRAYER

Ask Him to guard and protect you from becoming a spiritual casualty. Express to the Lord your full reliance on Him for spiritual security.

MOVE BEYOND LACK OF SPIRITUAL GROWTH

How carefully are you paying attention to maintaining and cultivating your relationship with Jesus Christ? What additional care do you need to take?

Your own reflections...personal application... personal prayer points...

The Master Arsonist

One year when wildfires swept through parts of Southern California, I noticed a photograph in the newspaper of an entire neighborhood leveled by the fires. All that was left were the foundations of the homes. But in the midst of all the burned, charred rubble stood one house that remained completely untouched, even by smoke. This gleaming white house stood in stark contrast to all of the ruin around it.

When asked why his house was left standing when all the others fell, the homeowner explained how he'd taken great care to make his house flame-retardant. This included double-paned windows, thick stucco walls, sealed eaves, concrete tile, and abundant insulation. Seeing this, the firefighters chose this spot to make their stand in fighting the fire. This man went the extra mile, and as a result, his house survived.

Today, our culture is being devastated by the wildfires of immorality. Satan, a master arsonist, is causing massive devastation. It destroys families and devastates relationships. And if we aren't careful, we could become its next victims.

> There is so much **immorality**.
> 1 CORINTHIANS 7:2 NIV

The writer of Proverbs asked, "Can a man scoop a flame into his lap and not have his clothes catch on fire?" (6:27 NLT). The answer is no. Fire can burn out of control so easily.

If we as believers allow temptation to infiltrate our lives and allow our sinful natures to prevail, we could fall as surely as a fire spreads if gasoline is thrown on it. But if we take practical steps to guard ourselves and stay close to the Lord, then we won't fall.

Let's go the extra mile to protect our homes and our lives against the wildfires of immorality.

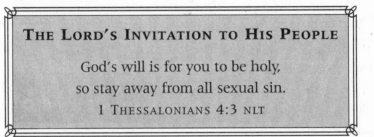

THE LORD'S INVITATION TO HIS PEOPLE

God's will is for you to be holy,
so stay away from all sexual sin.
1 THESSALONIANS 4:3 NLT

WITH GOD IN PRAYER

Ask Him to open your eyes to realize the full danger of the temptations that are most likely to entice you.

MOVE BEYOND THE HIGH RISK OF IMMORALITY

What dangerous temptations are encroaching upon your life? What action steps must you take to flee and avoid such temptation? What do you need to do to go the extra mile in protecting yourself and your children?

Your own reflections...personal application... personal prayer points...

Easy Prey

One has to go no further than Psalms to see the intimacy of David's relationship with God. It's so obvious that David loved God in a dear and tender way. And yet we know he fell into sin.

If you were to ask a group of Christians what they remember most from the life of David, the name Goliath would most likely come up. Another name probably would be mentioned as well—Bathsheba.

Goliath and Bathsheba represented David's greatest victory and his greatest defeat. Satan wasn't able to bring David down on the battlefield, so he defeated him in the bedroom. One evening, David laid eyes on Bathsheba, and very quickly he committed adultery with her.

> We are not **fighting** against flesh-and-blood enemies, but against **evil** rulers and authorities of the unseen world, **against** mighty powers in this dark world, and against evil **spirits** in the heavenly places.
>
> EPHESIANS 6:12 NLT

At this particular time in King David's life, we don't read about him worshiping the Lord. David had gotten away from intimacy with his God, and thus he was more vulnerable. He lowered his guard, and the moment he did so, he become an easy target for the devil.

Eventually, he confessed this sin and was forgiven. But he also reaped what he sowed. The sins he committed were repeated in the lives of his own children.

The devil continues to look for easy targets. He knows it's easier to hit something stationary than something that's on the move. Those who are moving forward in Christ, who are growing in their love for the Lord, aren't nearly as easy to hit as a person who has begun to relax his grip on the Lord. That's the one whom the devil will set his sights on. That's the one who will become his next casualty.

THE LORD'S INVITATION TO HIS PEOPLE

Stay alert! Watch out for your great enemy,
the devil. He prowls around like a roaring lion,
looking for someone to devour.
1 PETER 5:8 NLT

WITH GOD IN PRAYER

Take time to fully evaluate your heart and life before the Lord. In what ways have you fallen away from intimacy with Him and full dependence on Him?

MOVE BEYOND BEING AN EASY TARGET FOR THE DEVIL

In what ways have you relaxed your grip on the Lord? What must you do right now to tighten it?

Your own reflections...personal application... personal prayer points...

What's on Your Mind?

Sometimes people ask me to sign their Bibles, which isn't something I like to do, because I didn't write it. But when someone insists, I usually write the following inscription in his or her Bible: "Sin will keep you from this book, and this book will keep you from sin."

> If you **abide** in My word...
> you shall know the truth, and
> the **truth** shall make you free.
> JESUS, IN JOHN 8:31-32

I've found that sin will always keep you away from the Bible, because the devil wants to keep you out of God's Word. He doesn't care if you read magazines. He doesn't care if you watch television. He doesn't care if you read the latest novel on the bestseller list. He doesn't care if you watch movies. But the minute you pick up the Bible and crack it open, you'd better believe he'll try to distract you with everything he has. He doesn't want you to read it.

On the other hand, if you follow what the Bible teaches, it will keep you from sin. That's why we need to know the Bible. That's why we need to study it.

While it's a great idea to carry a Bible in your briefcase, pocket, or purse, the best place to carry it is in your heart. Know it well. Fill the memory banks God has given you with Scripture, because the devil will attack you in the realm of your mind. The best defense is a mind that's filled with God's Word.

THE LORD'S INVITATION TO HIS PEOPLE

Commit yourselves wholeheartedly to
these words of mine. Tie them to your hands
and wear them on your forehead as reminders.
Teach them to your children. Talk about
them when you are at home and when you
are on the road, when you are going to bed
and when you are getting up.

DEUTERONOMY 11:18–19 NLT

WITH GOD IN PRAYER

Talk with Him about what it means to you to abide in His Word.

MOVE BEYOND BEING UNFILLED
WITH GOD'S WORD

What steps should you take to increase your intake of God's Word and your heart's interaction with it?

Your own reflections...personal application... personal prayer points...

Giving God a Makeover

At first glance, the sins that brought the children of Israel down in the wilderness don't seem to have any rhyme or reason. But a closer examination reveals that the root problem was a lack of relationship with the true and living God.

When Moses was temporarily taken out of the scene when he went to meet with God on Mount Sinai, the people wanted something to take his place. It was only a matter of time until they were bowing before a golden calf.

When you get down to it, Moses was their first idol, and the golden calf was their second. Moses was like God to them, so when Moses was gone, they created a god of their own making.

> I looked, and **behold**, you had sinned against the LORD your God—had made for yourselves a molded calf! You had **turned aside** quickly from the **way** which the LORD had commanded you.
> DEUTERONOMY 9:16

We do the same when we start remaking God in our own image. When we give God a twenty-first-century makeover, when we make Him politically correct, when we start changing His Word to fit the perverted morals of our time, this becomes idolatry. We're remaking God because we aren't comfortable with what He says. We don't like His standards.

We try to remake God in our image so we can live the way we want to and do as we please. We want a celestial salad bar where we can casually stroll up, choose the attributes of God that most appeal to us, and leave the rest behind. It's religion à la carte.

Molding God and His Word into our image is as much an act of idolatry as the children of Israel's worshiping the golden calf.

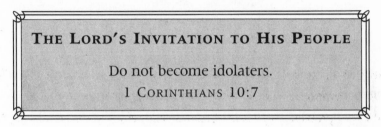

THE LORD'S INVITATION TO HIS PEOPLE

Do not become idolaters.

1 CORINTHIANS 10:7

WITH GOD IN PRAYER

Worship and praise Him for His holiness. Let Him know again that He deserves your complete devotion.

MOVE BEYOND REMAKING GOD IN OUR IMAGE

In what ways are you tempted to reinvent or transform God to fit what you want Him to be instead of worshiping and serving Him for who He really is?

Your own reflections...personal application... personal prayer points...

The Dangerous Question

The Bible tells us, "You shall not put the LORD your God to the test" (Deuteronomy 6:16 ESV). What does it mean to test God?

It's the mentality that asks the question, *As a Christian, how much can I get away with and still be saved? How far can I go and still be a child of God?* In other words, *How far to the edge can I get without falling off?* It's a dangerous question to ask.

The church at Corinth had developed a similar problem. It was located in a cosmopolitan city, with visitors coming from all around the world. The city of Corinth was entrenched in sin. Some of the believers there thought they could commit certain sins and still be acceptable to God. Paul had to set the record straight.

He wrote to them, "All things are lawful for me, but not all things are helpful; all things are lawful for me, but not all things edify" (1 Corinthians 10:23).

> We must not put Christ to the **test,** as some of them did and were **destroyed** by serpents.
> 1 CORINTHIANS 10:9 ESV

Let's not push the limits and see how much we can get away with as believers. Let's go the other direction. Instead, let's ask, *How much more fully can I know this One who died for me and forgave me and has done so much on*

*my behalf? How can I become more like Him? How can I make an impact in my
world for Him?*

Let's not take for granted all that God has done for us in our lives. May
we never see how far we can go and be guilty of testing the Lord. Rather, let's
stay as close to Him as we possibly can.

THE LORD'S INVITATION TO HIS PEOPLE

Whatever you do in word or deed,
do all in the name of the Lord Jesus,
giving thanks to God the Father through Him.

COLOSSIANS 3:17

WITH GOD IN PRAYER

Make this your request: "Lord, show me how I can know You more deeply.
Show me how I can become more like You. Show me how I can make an
impact in my world for You."

MOVE BEYOND TAKING GOD'S
GRACE FOR GRANTED

What has the strongest pull in your life—Christ or the brink of sin?

Your own reflections...personal application...
personal prayer points...

Conditional Obedience

My dog practices selective listening. When he doesn't like what I'm saying, he acts as though he doesn't understand me. If he's in my room at bedtime and I tell him to leave, he looks at me as if to say, "What?" It's as though his hearing is gone.

On the other hand, he can be asleep somewhere in the house, and if I go downstairs, open the cupboard, and pull out his leash, he suddenly has supersonic hearing. He's right there at my side.

When he likes what I want him to do, my dog hears and obeys me. But when he doesn't like what I want him to do, my dog doesn't hear and doesn't obey.

We can be the same with God. When God tells us to do something we like, we answer, "Yes, Lord!" When He tells us to stop doing something, we respond, "God, I think you're cutting out on me. I'm not hearing you clearly."

> They did not **obey** or incline their
> ear, but followed the counsels and
> the dictates of their evil **hearts**,
> and went **backward** and not forward.
> JEREMIAH 7:24

Jesus said, "You are My friends if you do whatever I command you" (John 15:14). He didn't say, "You are My friends if you do the things you personally agree with." God has told us in His Word how we're to live. It's not for us to pick and choose sections of the Bible we like and toss the rest aside.

If God tells you to do something, He says it for good reason, and you need to obey Him. If God says not to do something, He also says it for good reason. Even if you don't understand it, obey Him.

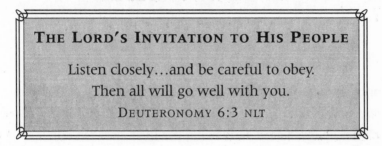

THE LORD'S INVITATION TO HIS PEOPLE

Listen closely...and be careful to obey.
Then all will go well with you.
DEUTERONOMY 6:3 NLT

WITH GOD IN PRAYER

Thank the Lord Jesus for the friendship with Him that is ours as we fully obey Him.

MOVE BEYOND DISOBEDIENCE

What has God told you to do that you have been resisting? Whatever it is, obey Him now.

Your own reflections...personal application... personal prayer points...

What's Inside?

I heard the story of a pastor who boarded a bus one Monday morning, paid his fare, and took his seat. A few minutes later, he realized the driver had given him too much change. Some people might have put it in their pocket and said, *Lord, thank You for Your provision.* But this pastor knew that would be wrong. At the next stop, he walked to the front of the bus with the extra change and said to the driver, "Excuse me, sir, you gave me too much change, and I wanted to return it to you, because obviously you made a mistake."

The driver said, "Pastor, I didn't make a mistake. I was at your church last night and heard you preach on honesty. I wanted to see if you practice what you preach." Fortunately, he did.

People are watching you as a Christian. They're scrutinizing your every move. You should know they aren't hoping you'll be a godly witness; they're hoping you'll slip up so they'll have something on which to conveniently hang their doubts and unbelief.

> My righteousness I **hold** fast, and will not let it go; my heart shall not **reproach** me as long as I live.
>
> JOB 27:6

Humorist Will Rogers said we should live in such a way that we wouldn't mind selling our pet parrot to the town gossip. That's the idea of integrity—having nothing in our lives to be ashamed of. This personal integrity is something we're developing on a daily basis with every thought we think and every action we take. We're either building up character or tearing it down.

What kind of character do you have? Who are you in private? For all practical purposes, that's the real you.

THE LORD'S INVITATION TO HIS PEOPLE

Walk before Me...in integrity of heart
and in uprightness.

1 KINGS 9:4

WITH GOD IN PRAYER

Thank Him for how thoroughly God sees the real you—even the things that you may be trying to hide from others.

MOVE BEYOND A SHORTAGE OF INTEGRITY

How would you describe the kind of person you are in private, when you're alone? What is your real character? What are you doing to build up your character?

Your own reflections...personal application... personal prayer points...

The Spiritual Battlefield

Someone once asked the great evangelist Charles Finney, "Do you really believe in a literal devil?" Finney responded, "Try opposing him for a while, and you'll see if he's literal or not."

If you want to find out if there really is a devil, start walking with Jesus Christ and seeking to live fully in the will of God. You'll find just how real Satan is.

I think many people, after they've decided to follow Christ, are surprised to find that the Christian life is not a playground but a battleground. It isn't a life of ease, but one of conflict, warfare, and opposition.

The question facing us is simple: on the spiritual battlefield, will we be victorious or will we be victims?

> In the world you will have tribulation; but be of good **cheer**, I have **overcome** the world.
>
> JESUS, IN JOHN 16:33

It's been said you can tell a lot about a man by who his enemies are. The same is true for us. We're no longer opposing God, but we now have a new and powerful foe, and he's described in the Bible as the devil. The devil, of course, isn't happy with the fact that he has lost one of his own. He's angry that you've surrendered your life to Jesus Christ. Now you've become a potential threat to his kingdom.

The closer you stay to the Lord, the safer you are, because you stand in the work Jesus did on the Cross. Don't try to engage the devil in your own ability, because he can chew you up and spit you out. But if you stand in the Lord and in His power, and if you stay as close to Him as you can, you'll be safe.

THE LORD'S INVITATION TO HIS PEOPLE

Let him who thinks he stands
take heed lest he fall.
1 CORINTHIANS 10:12

WITH GOD IN PRAYER

Thank Him specifically for His triumphant power over our enemy, the devil.

MOVE BEYOND BEING THE DEVIL'S LIKELIEST VICTIM

How can you stay closer to God today and enjoy His security?

Your own reflections...personal application... personal prayer points...

Power with a Purpose

What comes to mind when you hear the word *dynamite*? I automatically think of something explosive. And when something is described as dynamic, I know it's something unusual or special, something that stands out.

Jesus told the disciples they would receive power when the Holy Spirit came upon them. The word Jesus used for power is from the Greek word *dunamis,* the same word from which we get our words *dynamite* and *dynamic.*

> You will receive **power** when the Holy Spirit comes upon you. And you will be my witnesses, telling **people** about me everywhere—in Jerusalem, throughout Judea, in Samaria, and to the **ends** of the earth.
>
> JESUS, IN ACTS 1:8 NLT

Power is exciting if it is used for something productive. Have you ever seen a fire hose on the loose? It can knock people over. It can be very destructive. But if you get hold of it and aim it in the right direction, you can do a lot of good.

In the same way, God has given us the power of the Holy Spirit for a purpose. God's power is practical. He didn't give us the Holy Spirit so we would behave strangely. He gave us the Holy Spirit so we would be His witnesses, effectively sharing our faith. It's power with a purpose.

When the Holy Spirit came upon those first-century believers on the Day of Pentecost, the Bible says about three thousand people made commitments to Jesus Christ (see Acts 2:41). Peter made an important statement about the Holy Spirit on that occasion. He said the power they'd received was available not only to them but also to future generations of believers—"to you and to your children, and to all who are afar off" (Acts 2:39).

This means that the same power that changed their world is available to us to change our world.

THE LORD'S INVITATION TO HIS PEOPLE

Not by might, nor by power, but by my Spirit,
says the LORD of hosts.

ZECHARIAH 4:6 ESV

WITH GOD IN PRAYER

Praise Him for His power, and thank Him for making it available to us through the Holy Spirit.

MOVE BEYOND A SHORTAGE OF POWER

Empowered by the Holy Spirit of God, what should be your words and actions today as a witness of Jesus Christ in your world?

Your own reflections...personal application... personal prayer points...

Sowing
and Reaping

A successful building contractor called in one of his employees, a skilled carpenter, and told him he was putting him in charge of the next house the company was building. He instructed the carpenter to order all the materials and oversee the entire process from the ground up.

The carpenter excitedly accepted his assignment. It was his first opportunity to actually oversee an entire building project. He studied the blueprints and checked every measurement. Then he thought, *If I'm really in charge, why can't I cut a few corners, use less expensive materials, and put the extra money in my pocket? Who would know the difference? After we paint the place, no one would be able to tell.*

The carpenter set about his scheme. He used second-grade lumber and ordered inexpensive concrete for the foundation. He put in cheap wiring. He cut every corner he possibly could, but he reported the use of higher-quality building materials.

> He who sows to his flesh will
> of the flesh **reap** corruption, but
> he who sows to the Spirit will of
> the **Spirit** reap everlasting life.
> GALATIANS 6:8

When the home was completed, he asked his boss to come and see it. His boss quickly looked it over and said, "You've been such a good and faithful worker and have been so honest all of these years, I'm showing my gratitude by giving this house to you."

We will reap what we sow. Just as we can't plant weeds and reap flowers, we can't sin and reap righteousness. There are reactions to our actions.

Think about it: every day, we're either sowing to the Spirit or we're sowing to the flesh. What kind of seeds will you sow today?

THE LORD'S INVITATION TO HIS PEOPLE

Sow for yourselves righteousness;
reap in mercy; break up your fallow ground,
for it is time to seek the LORD, till He comes
and rains righteousness on you.

HOSEA 10:12

WITH GOD IN PRAYER

Thank Him for the rewards He has promised you in full recognition of the things you do in this life (see 2 Corinthians 5:10).

MOVE BEYOND SOWING WEEDS

Where have you been cutting corners in carrying out the responsibilities God has given you? What corrections do you need to make in order to continue sowing seeds of righteousness—instead of weeds of worthlessness?

Your own reflections...personal application... personal prayer points...

Temporary Pleasures

There's a story in the Bible about a man named Esau who gave up everything for a little temporary pleasure. As the firstborn, Esau had been given the family birthright, which meant that one day he would be the spiritual leader of his family and would be in the ancestral line of the Messiah. But Esau didn't seem to care much about that. One day, his brother, Jacob, came along and proposed a trade: Esau's birthright for some stew Jacob was cooking. It sounded like a good deal to Esau at the time, because he was so hungry.

Later he realized how cheaply he'd sold out. But it was too late.

Esau had no regard for spiritual things—and there are a lot of people like that today. They couldn't care less about God until they're in a bind or until some tragedy hits. Then suddenly and miraculously, they have time for God. But when the crisis is past, they return to their old ways.

> A person is a **fool** to store
> up earthly wealth but not have a
> rich **relationship** with God.
> JESUS, IN LUKE 12:21 NLT

Jesus spoke about a farmer whose crop had produced generously. The farmer decided to tear down his barns and build larger ones to store everything. That way he could say to himself, "You have enough stored away for years to come. Now take it easy! Eat, drink, and be merry!" (Luke 12:19 NLT). But God told him, "You fool! You will die this very night. Then who will get everything you worked for?" (verse 20).

Are things on this earth more important to you than treasures in heaven? Everything you may hold dear will be left behind one day. And the only thing that will matter is what's waiting in heaven for you.

THE LORD'S INVITATION TO HIS PEOPLE

Do not lay up for yourselves treasures
on earth...but lay up for yourselves
treasures in heaven.
JESUS, IN MATTHEW 6:19–20

WITH GOD IN PRAYER

Think about the heavenly treasures that are yours in Christ Jesus, and thank and praise Him for these.

MOVE BEYOND ATTACHMENT TO WORLDLY RICHES

What are the earthly treasures or pleasures that have the most value to you and could therefore be hardest for you to give over to God? In your thinking, how do these compare with the treasures that are yours in heaven?

Your own reflections...personal application... personal prayer points...

The Peril of Prayerlessness

The Bible's first recorded prayer from Jacob is found in Genesis 32:9–12. Prior to this point, seven chapters of Genesis have been devoted to Jacob's life with no mention of prayer on his part.

That fact makes me wonder if Jacob ever prayed during that time. It's possible he did, but the Bible doesn't specifically mention it. It may have been Jacob's lack of prayer and lack of dependence on God that made him feel as though he had to manipulate his circumstances, as we see throughout those chapters.

It was commendable that Jacob was finally reaching out to God in Genesis 32, and there are even some good things about his prayer. He acknowledged the God of Abraham and Isaac as the true God. He confessed his own unworthiness. He brought his petition to the Lord. But it would have been better if he'd said, "Lord, what should I do now?" Instead, he apparently decided what he was going to do, then asked God to bless it. Jacob wanted what was right, but he went about it in the wrong way.

> Deliver me, I pray, from the **hand** of
> my brother, from the hand of Esau; for
> I fear him, lest he **come** and attack me
> and the mother with the **children**.
> GENESIS 32:11

Is that not like us? We make our plans, then ask God to bless them. But that isn't really what God has in mind for our prayers to Him. Instead, we should pray along these lines: *Lord, give me wisdom from your Word and from godly people who will guide me biblically. Help me do the right thing.*

God helps those who can't help themselves. This is what Jacob needed to realize. Let's learn to seek out God's will rather than bypass it.

THE LORD'S INVITATION TO HIS PEOPLE

Pray like this:... May your will be done
on earth, as it is in heaven.
JESUS, IN MATTHEW 6:9–10 NLT

WITH GOD IN PRAYER

Let this be your prayer: *Lord, give me wisdom from your Word and from godly people who will guide me biblically. Help me do the right thing.*

MOVE BEYOND PRAYERLESSNESS

In what current pursuits or responsibilities in your life have you been guilty of asking God simply to bless your own plans—rather than truly seeking out His guidance first?

Your own reflections...personal application... personal prayer points...

God's Way

It's interesting how God came to different people in the Bible.

To Abraham, God came as a traveler. Abraham was outside his tent when three messengers arrived. Two were angels, while one was God Himself. Why did the Lord come to Abraham as a sojourner? Because a sojourner is what Abraham was.

The night before the Israelites began their siege of Jericho, God came to Joshua, the commander of Israel's armies, as Commander of the Lord's army.

> To the **faithful** you show
> yourself faithful; to those with
> **integrity** you show integrity. To the
> pure you show yourself **pure**, but to
> the wicked you show yourself hostile.
> PSALM 18:25-26 NLT

When God came to Jacob, He came as a wrestler, and Jacob wrestled with Him. Why? Jacob was always fighting, conniving, resisting, and wrestling to get what he wanted.

Maybe you can relate to Jacob. Maybe there's something you want from God, even a good thing, like the salvation of a husband or wife. Maybe you're tired of being single and want to get married. Or maybe you want to serve God in a ministry.

Don't resort to conniving to get what you want—because you may get it, but at a great cost. Jacob got what he wanted and paid dearly for it. I believe if he'd waited on God, he would have received what he needed and what God had promised.

God wants to do His will in our lives in His way and in His time. If you need something from God, be patient and wait on Him. God will meet you wherever you are to lift you to where He wants you to be.

THE LORD'S INVITATION TO HIS PEOPLE

Wait on the LORD; be of good courage,
and He shall strengthen your heart;
wait, I say, on the LORD!

PSALMS 27:14

WITH GOD IN PRAYER

Acknowledge before Him your willingness to wait on His timing and choices in every area of your life.

MOVE BEYOND CONNIVING WITH GOD

In what area of life—in what needs and desires—do you especially need to be patient right now as you wait on God to act? What kind of "conniving" are you tempted to want to try? How can you avoid that wrong response?

Your own reflections...personal application... personal prayer points...

Revive Us Again!

Have you ever felt like you're out there all alone as a Christian? Sometimes it may seem that you're the only one who's serving the Lord or speaking up for Him at your workplace or school—especially if other Christians you know are afraid to stand up and be counted as such.

As dark as things are, remember this: "When the enemy comes in like a flood, the Spirit of the LORD will raise up a standard against him" (Isaiah 59:19). This is good news. When things are really wicked, when things are really dark, you can anticipate that God will do something.

That's why, as I look at the way things are going in these days, I'm praying and hoping for a work of God in our generation.

> Will You not **revive** us again,
> that Your people may rejoice in You?
> PSALM 85:6

When you look back at the great revivals in history, in Bible times and otherwise, you find five traits that are true of every revival:

1. They began during a time of national depression and deep moral distress.
2. They usually began with an individual, someone whom God would work on or work through. It may have been someone who prayed or someone who preached.
3. They were built on the bold preaching and teaching of the Word of God and obedience to His Word.

4. They brought about an awareness of sin and the need to repent of it.

5. They brought about a change in the moral climate; something happened in the culture as a result.

When God is forgotten, a moral breakdown soon follows. But doing what God wants us to do will have a positive impact on our culture.

THE LORD'S INVITATION TO HIS PEOPLE

Return to the LORD your God, for you
have stumbled because of your iniquity.

HOSEA 14:1

WITH GOD IN PRAYER

Ask Him to use you in the work of revival—that He will work on you and through you.

MOVE BEYOND OUR MORAL BREAKDOWN

What exactly does God want you to do now in order to have a godly impact on our culture?

Your own reflections...personal application... personal prayer points...

In Search of Ordinary People

God uses ordinary people to do extraordinary things. While we're looking for some great superstar to come on the scene, God is developing someone in obscurity whom we haven't ever heard of. We'll think of some celebrity and say, "What if so-and-so became a Christian? Wouldn't that be wonderful?" And while we're wondering if so-and-so will ever come around, God is grooming someone unknown to us.

Think of the time when a giant Philistine was taunting the armies of Israel. Everyone was paralyzed with fear. So whom did God select? He chose a shepherd boy who had been sent by his father to take food to his brothers on the front lines. That boy went out to face the giant with a few stones, a sling, and—most important—faith in God. And that person God used—David—defeated Goliath.

> People judge by **outward** appearance,
> but the LORD looks at the heart.
> 1 SAMUEL 16:7 NLT

At another time in Israel's history when God's people were immobilized by fear because of their enemies, He found a guy threshing wheat and called him to go and rescue Israel. The man was convinced God had called up the wrong guy. But God selected him because he didn't trust in his own ability. Gideon had to trust in God—and he became the leader in Israel's defeat of their enemies.

If you have faith in God, if you believe God can use you, if you're willing to take a step of faith here and there, then God can do incredible things through you.

God isn't looking for ability, but availability. He can give you ability in time. God is looking for someone who will say, *I would like to make a difference where I am. Lord, I'm available.* Pray that way…then watch what God will do.

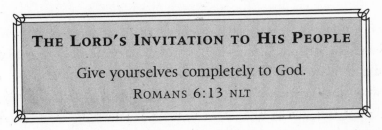

THE LORD'S INVITATION TO HIS PEOPLE

Give yourselves completely to God.
ROMANS 6:13 NLT

WITH GOD IN PRAYER

Talk honestly with God about your faith in Him to use you.

MOVE BEYOND BEING UNAVAILABLE TO GOD

What proof is there in your life that you're truly available to God to be used for His purposes?

Your own reflections...personal application... personal prayer points...

Salt and Light

I think we Christians are sometimes tempted to isolate ourselves. We want to submerge ourselves in Christian subculture and not get too involved in the world. But Jesus said, "You are the salt of the earth."

When Jesus made that statement to His disciples so long ago, they understood the significance of what He was saying. The analogy can be lost on us today because we don't know what it means.

In those days, salt was highly valuable. In fact, the Romans considered salt more important than the sun itself. Sometimes Roman soldiers would even be paid with salt. So when Jesus told His followers, "You are the salt of the earth," He was saying in a sense, "You're valuable. You're important. You're significant. You can make a difference."

Stop and think about salt. It really can do a lot. A little salt on a bland piece of meat can make it tastier. Have you ever had someone put salt in your water when you weren't looking? You immediately noticed the change. A little pinch of salt can alter the flavor of something, just as one Christian in a situation can effect change.

> You are the **salt** of the earth.
> But what good is salt if it has
> lost its **flavor**?... You are the
> light of the world—like a city on
> a **hilltop** that cannot be hidden.
> JESUS, IN MATTHEW 5:13-14 NLT

Likewise Jesus says, "You are the light of the world." Have you ever been in a dark room and someone turned on a flashlight? The light wasn't hard to find, was it? In the same way, one believer who lets his or her light shine can really make a difference in this dark world.

God has singled you out to make a difference in the world—a strategic difference.

THE LORD'S INVITATION TO HIS PEOPLE

Let your light so shine before men,
that they may see your good works and
glorify your Father in heaven.

MATTHEW 5:16

WITH GOD IN PRAYER

Thank Him for our incredible privilege as Christians of being the salt of the earth and the light of the world.

MOVE BEYOND TOO LITTLE IMPACT IN YOUR WORLD

What can you do today to truly let your light shine?

Your own reflections...personal application... personal prayer points...

By the Brook

When the Bible says ravens brought Elijah food, it doesn't mean they took his order, flew through the local fast-food restaurant, then delivered his meal. Ravens are scavengers. They brought little bits of meat and bread to Elijah. What's more, the water in the brook from which he drank would have been somewhat polluted. It wasn't an easy situation.

How easily Elijah could have said, "Well, Lord, I don't really want to be in this crummy little place. I prefer being in front of people. I like the lime-light." But the Lord was preparing Elijah for something beyond his wildest dreams. Not long after this, Elijah would be standing on Mount Carmel in that great showdown with the false prophets (see 1 Kings 18:20–39).

> The ravens **brought** him bread and meat in the morning, and bread and **meat** in the evening; and he drank from the brook.
>
> 1 KINGS 17:6

Sometimes we don't like where God has put us. We say, *Lord, I don't care for this situation. I don't like where I am. I want to do something great for You. I want to make a difference in my world.* But the Lord wants you to be effective right where you are. He wants you to take advantage of the opportunities in front of you and be faithful in the little things. Who knows what God has in store for you in that place?

If God has you by some muddy little brook, so to speak, just hang in there. Be faithful, do what He has already asked of you, and wait on Him and on His timing. God will do something wonderful for you or with you. Just be available and open to do what He wants you to do.

THE LORD'S INVITATION TO HIS PEOPLE

Be of good courage,
and He shall strengthen your heart.
PSALM 31:24

WITH GOD IN PRAYER

Confess to God your openness to all that He wants to do in your life right now and your willingness to go—or stay—wherever He wants you.

MOVE BEYOND COMPLAINING
ABOUT WHERE GOD HAS YOU

What step of faithfulness to God's calling do you need to take today?

Your own reflections...personal application...
personal prayer points...

Between
Two Worlds

The Bible mentions a category of Christians who are described as carnal. These are people in a state of arrested spiritual development. They've never really grown up.

They're caught between two worlds: they have too much of the Lord to be happy in the world, but too much of the world to be happy in the Lord. They're the most miserable people around.

Many of us realize that this world doesn't have the answers to life's questions and can't be trusted. But at the same time, we don't trust God either. We haven't made a stand.

But it's time to say, "I believe in Jesus Christ." It's time to stand up for the truth and not just blend into the woodwork.

So often in our attempts to gain credibility, we lose our integrity. In our attempts to relate to people, we lose any power we might have had in relating to them, because we've compromised our principles.

> The righteous are **bold** as a lion.
> PROVERBS 28:1

The Bible gives us many examples of people who stood up for what was right at the risk of losing something important, even their lives. One such person was Daniel, who held a position of great influence in Nebuchadnezzar's court. Even so, he wouldn't compromise his principles.

Maybe you're afraid to stand up for Jesus Christ. You're afraid it could hurt your career or a relationship or something else. But God provides moments when we must take a stand for what we know is true.

When you stand for Jesus, you may be criticized, and you might even lose something important to you. But whatever you lose, God will make it up to you. He'll bless you for standing up for what's right.

> ## THE LORD'S INVITATION TO HIS PEOPLE
>
> Be strong in the Lord
> and in the power of His might.
> EPHESIANS 6:10

WITH GOD IN PRAYER

Ask Him to make you strong when the times come for you to take a stand for Christ. Thank Him for the blessings He promises to those who are faithful in this.

MOVE BEYOND THE FEAR OF
STANDING FOR CHRIST

As you anticipate the days and weeks ahead, what opportunities to take a stand for Christ will you seize?

Your own reflections...personal application... personal prayer points...

Make Your Choice

Have you ever had one of those indecisive days? I'm usually decisive, but I can get in a mood where I just can't make a decision. I can be at the window of a take-out place and suddenly be stricken with indecision. That's not so tragic at a take-out window. But when people are indecisive with God, it's a serious problem.

> Elijah came to all the **people**,
> and said, "How long will you
> **falter** between two opinions?
> If the Lord is God, follow Him."
> 1 Kings 18:21

That's how it was with Israel in Elijah's day. For many decades the nation had gone back and forth between false gods and the true God. Not wanting to be responsible or live under absolutes, they would follow some other god. When they reaped the results of following that god, they'd scurry back to the Lord and say they were sorry. But when their problems went away, they would go back like wayward children and do the same thing again.

Every time they were on the brink of destruction, God would be merciful and forgive them. But one day, Elijah basically said to them, "Enough is enough. Make a choice. Which side are you on?"

Moses had posed a similar choice to Israel when they worshiped the golden calf. He said, "Whoever is on the LORD's side—come to me!" (Exodus 32:26). Likewise, his successor, Joshua, challenged Israel with these words: "Choose for yourselves this day whom you will serve" (Joshua 24:15).

And Jesus said, "He who is not with Me is against Me, and he who does not gather with Me scatters abroad" (Matthew 12:30).

Jesus demands that we choose. He demands we decide which side we're on. Choose this day whom you will serve.

THE LORD'S INVITATION TO HIS PEOPLE

Choose today whom you will serve.

JOSHUA 24:15 NLT

WITH GOD IN PRAYER

Let Him know that you choose Him—and that you'll follow Him, no matter what it costs.

MOVE BEYOND INDECISIVENESS

What are the occasions or situations in which you struggle most with spiritual indecisiveness? What decisions and choices do you need to make?

Your own reflections...personal application... personal prayer points...

Lukewarm People

Milk is great cold. There's nothing quite like a cold glass of milk with a couple of cookies. Milk is also good hot. With a little Ovaltine, it's great. But lukewarm milk? The thought of it is sickening. It just doesn't cut it.

In Revelation 3, Jesus spoke of lukewarm individuals. He said, "I know all the things you do, that you are neither hot nor cold. I wish that you were one or the other!" (Revelation 3:15 NLT).

It's interesting here that Jesus said He would prefer either hot or cold. You would think He would have said, "I would rather you be hot. But if lukewarm is all I can get, it's better than nothing." You would think lukewarm would be more acceptable to Him, because it's somewhat close to hot. But Jesus was, in effect, saying, "I don't want lukewarm. I don't want halfhearted commitments. I want you to decide. I want you totally in, or I would rather you were totally out."

> I know all the things you do, that you are neither **hot** nor **cold**. I wish that you were one or the other! But since you are like lukewarm water, neither hot nor cold, I will **spit** you out of my mouth!
>
> JESUS, IN REVELATION 3:15-16 NLT

Here's why. We know that being hot is good—you're on fire, you're walking with God, you're where God wants you to be. But if you're cold, hopefully you'll at least realize you're cold and one day realize your need for Christ and come to Him. The lukewarm person, however, is worse off than the cold person because he's self-deceived. The lukewarm person says, "I go to church. I read the Bible sometimes. I kind of believe in God—when it's convenient." That's the worst state of all.

What is your spiritual temperature today?

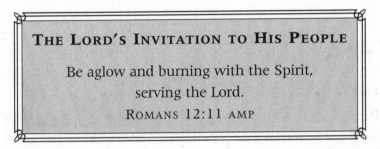

THE LORD'S INVITATION TO HIS PEOPLE

Be aglow and burning with the Spirit,
serving the Lord.
ROMANS 12:11 AMP

WITH GOD IN PRAYER

Talk with Him about your spiritual temperature, and praise Him that in His holiness He expects nothing less than heat.

MOVE BEYOND LUKEWARMNESS

If your spiritual temperature needs more heat, what will it take to get it?

Your own reflections...personal application... personal prayer points...

His Representative

It's hard for many Christians to understand how suddenly their friends and family can turn against them, simply because they're now following Jesus Christ. People they've been close to for years suddenly become hostile.

I'm amazed at how even parents have turned against children. I've heard teens and young adults tell me how they were strung out on drugs or living sexually permissive lives or getting in trouble all the time with the law. Then they found Christ, and their lives changed. They began living moral lives. Yet their parents were angry with them for coming to faith when, in fact, they should have been elated by the change.

Sometimes even parents won't understand what the Lord is doing in their child's life. Or children won't understand the miraculous work God is doing in their parents. Sometimes it's the same situation between husband and wife, or among friends or co-workers. They just don't understand.

> Remember the word that I said to you,
> "A servant is not greater than his
> **master.**" If they **persecuted** Me,
> they will also persecute you.
> JOHN 15:20

Remember when Saul (later to become the apostle Paul) was striking out against Christians? One day on the Damascus Road, he met none other than Jesus Christ Himself, who asked him, "Saul, Saul, why are you persecuting Me?" (Acts 9:4). Saul thought his fight had been against Christians, but it was against Christ Himself.

People take their hostilities out on you because you're God's representative. I've spoken with people who, when they discover I'm a pastor, suddenly begin dumping on me everything they have against God. I've come to realize this happens because I'm God's representative, just as all believers are.

It's a great honor to be His representative. But with that honor comes responsibility. Be careful. Don't keep someone away from Christ by misrepresenting Him.

THE LORD'S INVITATION TO HIS PEOPLE

Be very careful...making the most
of every opportunity.
EPHESIANS 5:15–16 NIV

WITH GOD IN PRAYER

Thank Him for making it clear in His Word that believers in Christ are to expect persecution for His Name's sake. Thank Him for this honor and privilege.

MOVE BEYOND CARELESSNESS
IN HOW YOU REPRESENT CHRIST

You can misrepresent Christ by becoming angry or upset when you face hostility or persecution for your faith. What can help you keep from doing this?

Your own reflections...personal application... personal prayer points...

The Faithful Follower

Near the end of his life, the apostle Paul wrote to the young pastor Timothy, "I have fought the good fight, I have finished the race, I have kept the faith" (2 Timothy 4:7). A few sentences later, he referred to a man named Demas who had deserted him, "having loved this present world, and has departed for Thessalonica" (verse 10). When it got too hard for Demas, he quit. He didn't want to be a follower of Jesus if it required anything of him, if it cost him anything, and certainly if it meant he would suffer persecution.

> Whoever **denies** Me before men, him I will also deny before **My Father** who is in heaven.
> JESUS, IN MATTHEW 10:33

Jesus spoke of the same dilemma in the parable of the sower, in which He compared the Word of God entering the hearts of men and women to seeds a farmer scatters. Jesus explained,

He who received the seed on stony places, this is he who hears the word and immediately receives it with joy; yet he has no root in himself, but endures only for a while. For when tribulation or persecution arises because of the word, immediately he stumbles. (Matthew 13:20–21)

There are some who will abandon their Christian faith when trouble comes or persecution arises. They give up. They deny the Lord. One way people do this is by simply saying, "I don't know Him." But another way is to not confess your faith in Jesus Christ or speak up for Him when the opportunity arises.

Do people know you're a Christian? Do your co-workers know you're a Christian? Do your family members know you're a follower of Jesus Christ? Are you speaking up for Him? I hope so.

> ## The Lord's Invitation to His People
>
> Arise, shine; for your light has come!
> And the glory of the LORD is risen upon you.
> ISAIAH 60:1

WITH GOD IN PRAYER

Ask Him for boldness in being a witness for the Lord Jesus Christ.

MOVE BEYOND FAILURE TO WITNESS FOR CHRIST

Do the unbelievers around you know you're a Christian? If not, how and when should you let them know?

Your own reflections...personal application... personal prayer points...

Ingratitude

A man was on the roof of a three-story house, nailing down a loose shingle. He lost his footing and began to slip. As he began sliding down the roof, he was terrified at the thought of falling to his death. He started shouting, "God, help me! I'm falling! God, do something!"

As he came to the edge of the roof, his belt loop caught on a nail and stopped him long enough for him to grab hold again. He called out, "It's okay, God, I don't need You after all. I got caught on a nail."

That's how we can be sometimes. We cry out to God. He answers our prayers. Then we say, *It's okay, God. Everything seemed to work out.* But do we ever stop and realize how God worked through various circumstances to come to our rescue?

We need to put as much zeal into thanking God for what He has done as we put into pleading with God when we're in need.

> Although they knew God, they did not glorify Him as God, nor were **thankful**, but became **futile** in their thoughts, and their foolish hearts were darkened.
> ROMANS 1:21

I heard about a hospital chaplain who kept a record of some two thousand patients whom he'd visited who were in life-threatening conditions. All showed signs of repentance. But among those restored to health, only two showed a marked change in their spiritual lives after their recovery. In other words, when these people thought they would die, they repented. But when they recovered, they forgot about God. They obviously had no true appreciation for the recovery He had granted them.

What would you think of a person who always wanted things from you but never offered a word of thanks in return? We can be that way with God, can't we? Let's remember to always thank Him.

THE LORD'S INVITATION TO HIS PEOPLE

Give thanks for everything to God the Father
in the name of our Lord Jesus Christ.
EPHESIANS 5:20 NLT

WITH GOD IN PRAYER

Take plenty of time to thank God for His countless gifts and blessings in your life. Mention them specifically.

MOVE BEYOND INGRATITUDE

How can you make sure that thankfulness to God is a permanent attitude in your heart and mind?

Your own reflections...personal application... personal prayer points...

When Praise Becomes a Sacrifice

There are times when it's a sacrifice to offer praise to God because, quite frankly, we don't really want to praise Him. There are times when we're down or depressed because things aren't going that well, and we don't really feel like praising the Lord.

Yet the Bible is filled with admonitions to give glory and praise and thanks to God. Like this one: "Praise the LORD! Oh, give thanks to the LORD, for He is good! For His mercy endures forever" (Psalm 106:1).

Notice that this verse doesn't tell us to give thanks to God when we feel good, but to give thanks because He is good. I don't praise Him because I feel like it. I praise God because He's worthy of that praise, regardless of what I'm going through.

I should praise Him for no other reason than that God tells me to. And I've discovered that when I begin to praise the Lord simply out of obedience, in time the emotion begins to engage with my act of obedience

> Whoever offers **praise**
> glorifies Me.
> PSALM 50:23

In the gospel of Luke, we find the story of ten men who were miraculously touched by Jesus. Because these men had leprosy, they were outcasts from society. Yet Jesus went out of His way to touch them and heal them of this dread disease. Only one, a Samaritan, returned and gave thanks and praise to God.

Jesus asked, "Were there not any found who returned to give glory to God except this foreigner?" (Luke 17:18).

In many ways, I think He's still asking this question today.

THE LORD'S INVITATION TO HIS PEOPLE

Let us continually offer the sacrifice
of praise to God, that is, the fruit of our lips,
giving thanks to His name.

HEBREWS 13:15

WITH GOD IN PRAYER

Think about how truly good God is, and give praise to Him.

MOVE BEYOND A LACK OF PRAISE FOR GOD

What can help you be more consistent in the habit of praising God?

Your own reflections...personal application... personal prayer points...

Not Ashamed

We're living in a time in which people stand up for all sorts of causes. We have people standing up for the rights of animals, for the environment, and for their right to perverse sexual lifestyles.

People stand up for everything imaginable, and in some cases, they're even willing to die for their cause. Although we may not agree with what they're saying in some cases, we have to admire their courage for believing in something so strongly they're willing to risk their reputations, their careers, and occasionally their very lives.

> I am not **ashamed** of the gospel of Christ,
> for it is the power of God to **salvation**
> for everyone who **believes**, for the
> Jew first and also for the Greek.
> ROMANS 1:16

Isn't it time we, as Christians, stand up for what we believe?

Romans 10:9 says, "If you confess with your mouth the Lord Jesus and believe in your heart that God has raised Him from the dead, you will be saved." What does it mean to confess the Lord Jesus? The very word *confess* gives us a clue. It means "to be in agreement with." When I'm confessing Jesus Christ, I'm not merely acknowledging that He existed, nor am I just acknowledging that He's God. When I confess Jesus Christ before others, I'm saying I agree with Him. It isn't enough to simply acknowledge that He has power and that He's moving in the lives of certain people. There must be a personal acknowledgment in which I've received Him as my own Savior and Lord.

In a day when so many are standing up for so many causes, it seems to me there are so many in the church who aren't standing up for anything. Let's be willing to stand up and confess Jesus Christ before others.

Isn't it time we, as Christians, stand up for what we believe? It's time to stand up and be counted.

THE LORD'S INVITATION TO HIS PEOPLE

Confess with your mouth the Lord Jesus.

ROMANS 10:9

WITH GOD IN PRAYER

Talk honestly with Him about anything that's holding you back from taking a stand for Christ. Ask Him to help you overcome these obstacles, and trust Him to do it as you fully rely on Him.

MOVE BEYOND FAILURE TO PUBLICLY CONFESS CHRIST

With confidence in the gospel's power, who do you need to talk with about salvation in Christ?

Your own reflections...personal application... personal prayer points...

Make the Right Choice

When I first became a Christian, I decided I would somehow find a way to live in two worlds. I was planning to hang out with my old friends and still be a Christian.

For a time, I was sort of in a state of suspended animation. I wasn't comfortable with my old buddies, but I wasn't quite comfortable with the Christians either. So I decided to be Mr. Solo Christian. I even said to my friends, "Don't worry about me. You're thinking I'll become a fanatic and carry a Bible and say, 'Praise the Lord.' It will never happen. I'm going to be cool about this. I'm going to believe in God now, but I won't embarrass you."

However, as God became more real to me and I began to follow Him more closely, He changed my life and my outlook, and my priorities began to change.

There are people who will discourage you from growing spiritually. They'll say, "I think it's good you're a Christian. I go to church too—at Christmas and Easter and for weddings. But you're getting a little too fanatical. You actually brought a Bible to work the other day. We were so embarrassed. You're no fun anymore. We're glad you've made changes in your life, but don't become too extreme." There are people like this who will discourage you.

> I have **chosen** the way of truth.
> PSALM 119:30

When this happens, you have the choice to either go with the flow or do what God wants you to do. Are you going to let people hold you back?

Are you going to let people discourage you from wholehearted commitment to Jesus Christ?

THE LORD'S INVITATION TO HIS PEOPLE

I have set before you life and death,
blessing and cursing; therefore choose life,
that both you and your descendants may live.

DEUTERONOMY 30:19

WITH GOD IN PRAYER

Ask Him to show you the specific choices you need to make right now as you follow the Lord Jesus Christ.

MOVE BEYOND WRONG PRIORITIES

How susceptible are you to being wrongly influenced by people who don't believe in Christ? How can you guard against their influence?

Your own reflections...personal application... personal prayer points...

After the Dove

The greatest challenges and temptations of the Christian life often come after great victories. I've found that after I experience great blessings in my life or after God works in a powerful way, the devil is there to challenge it all.

Think about it. After God had powerfully worked through Elijah on Mount Carmel, the prophet became so discouraged that he wanted to die. After Jesus was transfigured, He came down from the mountain to find a demon-possessed person waiting for Him.

Or think of Jesus being baptized in the Jordan River—the Holy Spirit came upon Him in the form of a dove, and God said, "This is my dearly loved Son, who brings me great joy" (Matthew 3:17 NLT). After such a spiritual high, Jesus was led into the wilderness to be tempted by the devil. After the dove came the devil.

> The thief's **purpose** is to steal and kill and destroy. My purpose is to give them a rich and **satisfying** life.
>
> JESUS, IN JOHN 10:10 NLT

The devil will always be there to challenge whatever God has done. He may come after church, after God has blessed you and spoken to you. You leave the parking lot and get hit with a heavy-duty temptation. You wonder how that could happen. But that's just the devil's way. He wants to make your life miserable. Most important, he wants to steal anything God has done in your life.

The devil is watching us, looking for vulnerabilities. That's why we need to pray for any person whom we know God is using. And that's why we need to brace ourselves. The more you step out to be used by the Lord, the more you can expect opposition from the devil.

THE LORD'S INVITATION TO HIS PEOPLE

Put on the whole armor of God, that you may be able to stand against the wiles of the devil.

EPHESIANS 6:11

WITH GOD IN PRAYER

Think about the Christians you know who are being used right now for the Lord, and pray for their protection from the devil's attacks.

MOVE BEYOND VULNERABILITIES TO THE DEVIL

How can you brace yourself against spiritual opposition? What defensive strategies can you adopt as you plan ahead?

Your own reflections...personal application... personal prayer points...

Getting to the Root

So often when something is going wrong in our country, we want to organize a boycott or protest. But did you know that as believers we have something more powerful than boycotts? It's called prayer—and the Bible tells us to devote ourselves to it: "Continue earnestly in prayer, being vigilant in it with thanksgiving" (Colossians 4:2).

We need to pray for our country. We need to pray for people who need to hear the gospel. And we need to share the gospel.

We need to share the good news of Jesus Christ with that woman who wants to abort her child. We need to share the gospel message with that man or woman who's trapped in the homosexual lifestyle. We need to share Christ with gang members. We need to share Him with all those in our society who are hurting.

> We use God's mighty weapons, not
> worldly weapons, to **knock down**
> the strongholds of human reasoning
> and to **destroy** false arguments.
> 2 CORINTHIANS 10:4 NLT

As people learn there's another kingdom, it will change the way they live in this one. Far too often, we Christians have been preoccupied with the symptoms in our society and haven't touched the root of the problem. The root is sin; the solution is the gospel.

So let's get to the root of our society's needs. Our society needs to turn back to God. We keep thinking that electing the right people to political office will solve all our problems, or some government program will solve them. But our problems won't be solved through any efforts of our own.

Only God can solve them. We need to turn back to Him.

Let's tell others about Christ and not be so preoccupied with what they're doing because of their sin. Let's try to reach people where they're really hurting. And let's always be sure we're praying.

THE LORD'S INVITATION TO HIS PEOPLE

Rescue those who are being taken away
to death; hold back those who are
stumbling to the slaughter.

PROVERBS 24:11 ESV

WITH GOD IN PRAYER

Thank Him for giving us the gospel as the full solution to every person's sin.

MOVE BEYOND WRONG RESPONSES
TO THE SIN AROUND YOU

Pray specifically for the unbelievers you know who need to hear and believe the gospel. When can you share the gospel with them?

Your own reflections...personal application... personal prayer points...

Simple Things

Have you ever wished you could do a miracle for friends or family members who aren't believers? You think, *If this happened, then they would believe.* We think it will take something dramatic or earthshaking. But so many times God works in simple ways to reach people.

For example, I read about a hardened atheist who had a young daughter. He didn't want her to believe in God. So one day, he wrote down the phrase *God is nowhere* on a piece of paper and told his little girl to read those words aloud.

She picked up the piece of paper. Since she was just learning to read, she slowly sounded out the words: "God…is…" She paused, studying the letters. "Oh, I understand, Daddy. 'God is now here'!"

The atheist was touched by that simple little event, and in time he became a believer in Jesus Christ.

> The **foolishness** of God is wiser than men, and the weakness of God is **stronger** than men.
> 1 CORINTHIANS 1:25

I'm reminded of a couple who attended one of our Harvest Crusades in Southern California. As they were walking down the street, they spotted a crumpled but colorful piece of paper on the ground. When they picked it up and smoothed it out, they discovered a Harvest Crusade flyer that contained a gospel message. They read it, then prayed and received Christ. They also went to the crusade and walked forward at the invitation. What a simple thing God used—a little crumpled piece of paper.

So often we think we need something dramatic to reach nonbelievers, or the greatest argument. But so often God does His work in totally unexpected ways.

God can use such simple things and speak in such simple ways. You just never know.

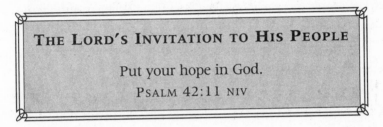

THE LORD'S INVITATION TO HIS PEOPLE

Put your hope in God.
PSALM 42:11 NIV

WITH GOD IN PRAYER

Thank God for the amazing and endlessly unique ways He reaches people.

MOVE BEYOND LIMITING GOD

Spend time in prayer, asking God to use you in surprising ways in the lives of unbelievers around you.

Your own reflections...personal application...
   personal prayer points...

Hearing God

There are people today who say they heard God telling them to follow a certain path of action, but that action doesn't align with Scripture's teaching. We must remember that God will never contradict His Word. He'll always lead us according to what the Bible says.

Some people come up with some lame concepts, such as "We're not married, but God has told us it's okay to have sex." I can assure them that God didn't say that, because in His Word He says, "Run from sexual sin.... For sexual immorality is a sin against your own body" (1 Corinthians 6:18 NLT). God will not contradict His Word.

Let's say you were expecting a letter from someone you're in love with or a response to a job application or something you ordered in the mail or the confirmation that you've won the lottery. You stand at the window, waiting for what seems like an eternity for the mail carrier to come by. Finally, he drives up, and you bolt over to your mailbox.

Would anything stop you from opening that piece of mail? Would you forget about actually reading what's inside it? Would you be content just to carry it around with you everywhere still unopened?

I doubt it. You probably would tear it open and read it before you even went back inside your house.

> Your **word** is a lamp to my feet
> and a **light** to my path.
> PSALM 119:105

The Bible is a written letter from God. A lot of us carry it around. We have it in different colors and sizes. We have it in different translations. But we never read it, even though it's a letter from God to us. It's just as if you had a handwritten note sent to you from God.

Without reading it, we'll never be able to say accurately, "Wow, God spoke to me!"

If you want God to speak to you, open up His Word.

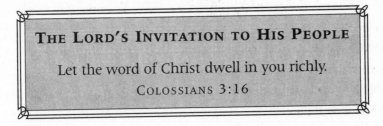

THE LORD'S INVITATION TO HIS PEOPLE

Let the word of Christ dwell in you richly.

COLOSSIANS 3:16

WITH GOD IN PRAYER

Thank Him that He's expressed His personal words to you in the Scriptures.

MOVE BEYOND NOT HEARING GOD SPEAK

Before God, make a solid commitment to spend daily time with Him by reading in His Word. Ask someone else (your spouse or a friend) to help keep you accountable in this commitment.

Your own reflections...personal application... personal prayer points...

The Voice of Circumstance

Not only does God speak to us through His Word, and not only will He never contradict His Word, but God also speaks through circumstances.

Although I'm not one to base major life decisions on circumstances alone, clearly there have been times when I've sensed that something was the will of God and then things fell into place circumstantially. At other times, circumstances have made it obvious that God was saying no.

A classic example of God speaking through circumstances was when God spoke to Gideon, who laid his fleece out on the ground, asking God to confirm His previous instructions.

> Gideon said to God, "If You will **save** Israel by my hand as You have said—look, I shall put a **fleece** of wool on the threshing floor; if there is dew on the **fleece** only, and it is dry on all the ground, then I shall **know** that You will save Israel by my hand, as You have said.
>
> JUDGES 6:36-37

Another example is Jonah, who certainly got the right message when God brought his journey to an abrupt halt, and Jonah found himself in the belly of a very large fish.

As a part of this process of leading us, God also speaks to us through people. There have been times when I've been listening to someone preach or have been talking with a friend, and suddenly what he's saying addressed perfectly the situation I was going through, even though the speaker was completely unaware of my circumstances. It made me realize that God Himself was speaking to me through those individuals.

Maybe God has spoken to you through a pastor or a Christian friend. Or perhaps He has been speaking to you through circumstances. Listen carefully... and weigh everything by Scripture, remembering that He'll never contradict His Word.

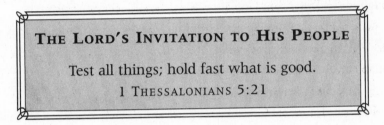

THE LORD'S INVITATION TO HIS PEOPLE

Test all things; hold fast what is good.

1 THESSALONIANS 5:21

WITH GOD IN PRAYER

Ask Him to lead you "in the paths of righteousness for His name's sake" (Psalm 23:3).

MOVE BEYOND UNAWARENESS OF HOW GOD SPEAKS

Think about the ways that God has led you in the past and what you have learned from those experiences. What principles can you identify for how God wants to guide you in the future?

Your own reflections...personal application... personal prayer points...

The Voice of Peace

Not only does God speak to us through His Word, and not only does He speak to us through people and circumstances, but God also speaks to us through His peace.

We're told, "Let the peace of God rule in your hearts, to which also you were called in one body; and be thankful" (Colossians 3:15). Another way to translate that verse is, "Let God's peace act as an umpire in your lives, settling with finality all matters that arise."

God's peace can act as an umpire in your life. He can settle with finality what you should do. Here's how it works. Maybe you think a certain course of action is the will of God for you. Circumstantially, things have fallen into place. You begin to proceed, but then you have a complete lack of peace. Something inside of you is saying, "Don't do it."

> You shall **go** out with joy,
> and be led out with **peace**.
> ISAIAH 55:12

The Old Testament tells the story of a clever group of individuals known as Gibeonites, who lived in Canaan. God had instructed Joshua not to make any deals with the inhabitants of the land. So the Gibeonites put on old shoes and clothes and pretended as though they'd come from a distant country. They told Joshua they had come to enter into an agreement with him. So Joshua unknowingly struck a deal with his enemies because he failed to consult the Lord.

Things can look good outwardly. Everything can seem right. Be careful. Learn to listen to that still, small voice. Learn to pay attention to the presence or lack of that peace in your life, because that's one of the ways God will lead you. When you're in the will of God, you'll have His peace.

> ### THE LORD'S INVITATION TO HIS PEOPLE
>
> Let the peace of God rule in your hearts.
> COLOSSIANS 3:15

WITH GOD IN PRAYER

Thank Him for the gift of His peace, and praise Him for being "the God of peace" (Romans 15:33).

MOVE BEYOND MISSING OUT ON GOD'S PEACE

What does "the peace of God" mean in your own experience? How would you describe it in order to help someone else understand it?

Your own reflections...personal application... personal prayer points...

When to Run

Some years ago, there was a story in the news about a man whose leg was trapped under a fallen tree. With no one around to come to his rescue, he took out a pocketknife and proceeded to amputate his leg. Then he made his way up the road, and someone picked him up and raced him to a hospital. Amazingly, this man with a severed leg still had enough presence of mind to tell the driver of the vehicle not to go too fast. He said, "I didn't come this far to die on the road. Take it easy."

I remember reading that story and thinking, "He did what? How could this guy cut off his leg? I would have laid under the tree and just waited for help." But the doctors who treated him later said that if he hadn't taken such a drastic measure, he would have died. He did it to save his life.

Sometimes we must take radical, drastic steps to remove ourselves from whatever it is that's hurting us spiritually. That may mean immediate change. It may mean physically getting up and saying, "I'm out of here." You might be attending that party. Watching that movie. Involved in that relationship. Traveling in that car. Wherever it is, you realize you shouldn't be there.

> **Run** from all
> these evil things.
> 1 TIMOTHY 6:11 NLT

God is convicting you. He's saying, "What are you doing here?" Don't be foolish. Just get up immediately and leave. That's not always possible, but most times it is.

Is there a relationship or a situation in which you don't belong? Has God been speaking to you about it? You'll be glad you took the time to listen.

> ## THE LORD'S INVITATION TO HIS PEOPLE
>
> Run from anything that stimulates youthful lusts. Instead, pursue righteous living, faithfulness, love, and peace.
> 2 TIMOTHY 2:22 NLT

WITH GOD IN PRAYER

Ask Him to show you clearly any relationship or situation you need to get out of.

MOVE BEYOND A FAILURE TO RUN

What radical, drastic step do you need to take to remove yourself from something that's hurting you spiritually?

Your own reflections...personal application... personal prayer points...

Seize Today

What kind of people does God want to use? We find the same pattern throughout Scripture: The people God used were faithful in what He placed before them. The people God used for big things were people who were faithful in little things.

Perhaps you've considered dedicating your life to Christian service one day, maybe even in another country. That's a good and noble aspiration. But how about just serving the Lord where you are right now? How about seizing the opportunities around you today?

> The **eyes** of the LORD run to and fro throughout the whole earth, to show Himself **strong** on behalf of those whose heart is loyal to Him.
>
> 2 CHRONICLES 16:9

Before David defeated Goliath, he was on an errand for his father, taking food to his brothers on the front lines. But as he was faithful in a little way, God gave him more. We know that when God called Gideon to lead Israel, Gideon was threshing wheat. When Elijah called Elisha into the Lord's service, Elisha was plowing a field. When Jesus called Peter and John to become fishers of men, they were mending their nets. Not one of them was sitting around thinking, "I wonder if God will ever do anything in my life?" They were busy with the work at hand.

While we're looking for distant opportunities, we might miss the ones that are right in front of us.

Are you serving the Lord right now with what He has called you to do? Be faithful in that. Do it well. Do it as unto the Lord. It may seem like your efforts go unnoticed, but there's Someone who sees. And He'll one day reward you openly.

THE LORD'S INVITATION TO HIS PEOPLE

Now therefore, fear the LORD, serve Him
in sincerity and in truth.... Serve the LORD!
JOSHUA 24:14

WITH GOD IN PRAYER

Ask God to open your eyes to the joy and privilege of serving Him in your daily responsibilities and situations.

MOVE BEYOND MISSING OUT
ON TODAY'S OPPORTUNITIES FROM GOD

What do you need to do today to ensure that you're faithful in serving the Lord?

Your own reflections...personal application...
personal prayer points...

Divine Discipline

Why does God bring tests into our lives? Is it because He wants to give us a hard time or embarrass us? No. It's because God wants us to learn. He wants us to mature spiritually. God wants us to learn to trust Him even when we don't understand Him. He wants us to be patient with Him even when He doesn't work according to our schedules.

The Bible says, "Whom the LORD loves He chastens" (Hebrews 12:6). Although God will discipline you when necessary, the word *chasten* also means "to train." God wants to teach you. He wants you to grow. He loves you so much He'll bring a series of tests and lessons into your life to whip you into shape. Those very tests, those very difficulties, and those very obstacles all can be indications of God's love for you.

> God blesses those who **patiently** endure testing and temptation. Afterward they will receive the **crown** of life that God has promised to those who **love** him.
>
> JAMES 1:12 NLT

When you start to cross the line and do something you shouldn't, God's Holy Spirit will be there to convict you. When you try to do something you know is wrong and God puts an obstacle in your path, it's because He loves you.

What you should be concerned about are the times when you do things you know are wrong and yet feel no remorse. But when you know something is wrong and struggle with it, that's a sign you're a child of God, and He loves you enough to show you when you're going astray.

Instead of seeing God's chastening as an intrusion in your life, welcome it. And be thankful He's looking out for you.

THE LORD'S INVITATION TO HIS PEOPLE

Don't reject the LORD's discipline,
and don't be upset when he corrects you.
For the LORD corrects those he loves, just as a
father corrects a child in whom he delights.
PROVERBS 3:11–12 NLT

WITH GOD IN PRAYER

Express your gratitude for the discipline He brings into your life.

MOVE BEYOND RESENTMENT OF GOD'S DISCIPLINE

What has God clearly protected you from because of the discipline He has brought into your life? Be aware of such things, and be thankful for your Father's consistent care for you.

Your own reflections...personal application... personal prayer points

The Trap of Temptation

Right after I became a Christian, other believers warned me, "Greg, watch out. There's a devil who will tempt you."

I said, "Right. A devil." I thought of the red figure with the pitchfork and horns.

They said, "No, the devil is real. He's a real spirit power, and he'll tempt you."

I said, "Get out of town. He isn't going to tempt me."

I was in high school at the time, and there was a certain girl in my art class whom I sort of had a crush on. I hadn't mustered up the courage to talk to her. I was sitting in class one day as a brand-new Christian, and suddenly she walked up to me and said, "Hi. What's your name?" We'd been in the same class for months, and she'd never even acknowledged my existence.

I told her my name. She said, "You know, you're kind of cute. I'm going up to the mountains this weekend. Why don't you just come up with me? Let's get to know each other better."

I thought, *This is it. This is what they told me about. It's temptation!*

I declined her invitation, knowing there had to be something behind it. I thought, *I'm not an idiot. No girl has ever come up to me and said this before. This is a set-up.*

Arm yourselves **before** the LORD for the war.
NUMBERS 32:20

That experience made me want to follow the Lord even more, because I saw the reality of the spiritual world beginning to unfold. Remember, the devil wants to keep you from coming to Christ. And once you've come to Christ, he wants to keep you from moving forward.

THE LORD'S INVITATION TO HIS PEOPLE

Submit to God. Resist the devil
and he will flee from you.

JAMES 4:7

WITH GOD IN PRAYER

Thank and praise Him for His power over all the forces of evil that can ever come against you.

MOVE BEYOND GETTING TRAPPED BY TEMPTATION

What have you learned about the reality of spiritual opposition and warfare? In this area, what are the most important things to keep in mind so that you can successfully overcome temptation?

Your own reflections...personal application... personal prayer points...

Spiritual Casualties

It's clear we're living in the last days. All around us, we see signs being fulfilled before our eyes that Jesus and the prophets told us to look for. The Bible warns that in the last days things would go from bad to worse (see 2 Timothy 3:1–13). The Scripture also warns that one of the signs of the last days will be a falling away from the faith, or an apostasy.

The question is, could you or I ever become one of those spiritual casualties? Could you or I ever fall away from the Lord? Without question, the inclination to sin is clearly within us. I have the potential to fall. You have it as well.

> The Holy Spirit tells us **clearly** that in the **last** times some will turn away from the true faith; they will follow deceptive spirits and **teachings** that come from demons.
> 1 TIMOTHY 4:1 NLT

This is why we must give careful attention to the potential pitfalls Scripture describes. We must be aware of certain things as we're living in the last days. We need to keep remembering what the apostle Paul wrote: "The night is almost gone; the day of salvation will soon be here" (Romans 13:12 NLT).

This is not a time to be playing games with God and living with a half-hearted commitment to Him. The only way to survive as a Christian and even flourish in these last days is to be completely committed to Jesus Christ.

Otherwise, we'll be easy targets for the tactics, strategies, and flaming arrows of the devil.

THE LORD'S INVITATION TO HIS PEOPLE

The night is almost gone; the day of salvation will soon be here. So remove your dark deeds like dirty clothes, and put on the shining armor of right living.

ROMANS 13:12 NLT

WITH GOD IN PRAYER

Bring before the Lord your genuine desire to thrive and flourish as a Christian.

MOVE BEYOND BEING A SPIRITUAL CASUALTY

Is your commitment to Jesus Christ complete? Evaluate your life to see if there is any area that needs to be turned over to His control.

Your own reflections...personal application... personal prayer points...

Living Victoriously

I remember reading a story about one of the battles between Gen. Lee and Gen. Grant during the Civil War. Gen. Lee was, of course, the head of the Confederate forces and was known for his brilliant tactics in doing a lot with a little. He didn't have the organization of the Union army or the manpower, but he was able to move in an effective way and foil his enemies on a number of occasions. His exploits had become so legendary that the Union soldiers were terrified of him.

One night, some Union soldiers were standing around the campfire talking about Gen. Lee. They said, "What if Gen. Lee does this? What are we going to do?"

Gen. Grant was standing a few feet away. He walked over and said to the soldiers, "The way you boys are talking, you would think Gen. Lee is going to do a somersault and land in the middle of our camp. Stop talking about what he's going to do, and let him worry about what we're going to do."

> When the enemy **comes** in like a flood, the Spirit of the LORD will lift up a **standard** against him.
> ISAIAH 59:19

Sometimes I see the same thing happening in the church: "Oh, the devil is doing this; the devil is doing that. Did you hear about this wicked thing that happened?"

I think we should stop focusing so much on what the devil is doing, and stop worrying so much about what he'll do, and instead let him worry about what we Christians will do.

Rather than trembling in fear about what the devil is doing, we can rejoice in the power God has given us to live victoriously and effectively for Him.

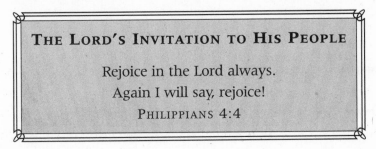

THE LORD'S INVITATION TO HIS PEOPLE

Rejoice in the Lord always.
Again I will say, rejoice!
PHILIPPIANS 4:4

WITH GOD IN PRAYER

Rejoice in the power He has given you to live victoriously and effectively for the Lord Jesus Christ.

MOVE BEYOND TOO MUCH FOCUS ON THE DEVIL

In what situations or circumstances are you most tempted to put too much focus on the devil? How can you avoid this temptation?

Your own reflections...personal application... personal prayer points...

The Little Things

When I was a kid, I collected snakes. I thought they were just great, and I had them in all colors and sizes.

I met a man who collected venomous snakes and had worked in a zoo. I really admired him. He'd been bitten by a tiger snake, which is the most deadly land snake on earth, even worse than a cobra. This man survived the snakebite because he'd been taking serum and had developed an immunity to the tiger snake's venom. As a result, this man basically thought he was indestructible, that no snake would ever take him down. He actually had cobras that hadn't been defanged slithering around loose in his house.

One day in his home, he was bitten by a cobra and didn't realize it until later when his leg began to swell. He was rushed to the hospital and died. This man thought that because he'd survived the tiger snake's bite, he didn't need to worry about cobras. That assumption became his downfall.

> Don't you realize that you become the **slave** of whatever you choose to **obey**? You can be a slave to sin, which leads to death, or you can **choose** to obey God, which leads to righteous **living**.
>
> ROMANS 6:16 NLT

Many times it's the little things that bring us down. Some Christians think, *I can handle this. I'm strong. I'll never fall.* But we need to be careful. When we feel the most secure in ourselves, when we think our spiritual lives are the strongest, our doctrine is the most sound, and our morals are the purest, we should be the most on guard and the most dependent on the Lord.

Sometimes the weakest Christian is in less danger than the strongest one, because our strongest virtues can become our greatest vulnerabilities.

> ### THE LORD'S INVITATION TO HIS PEOPLE
>
> Take up the whole armor of God,
> that you may be able to withstand in the
> evil day, and having done all, to stand.
> EPHESIANS 6:13

WITH GOD IN PRAYER

Thank Him for how He makes righteous living possible for us as we rely fully on His power and protection.

MOVE BEYOND SPIRITUAL OVERCONFIDENCE

What are the little things that seem to have the most harmful impact on your spiritual health and life? What strategy can you follow to lessen that impact?

Your own reflections...personal application... personal prayer points...

Cross Bearing

Sometimes we say, "We all have our crosses to bear. My cross is my supervisor at work," or, "My cross is my health problem," or, "My cross is a certain relative I don't get along with."

When we say that, we've lost the meaning of the Cross. If you were living in first-century Jerusalem and saw someone surrounded by Roman guards and carrying a cross down the street, there would be no question in your mind regarding where that person was going. You would know he was about to be taken outside of the city, laid on the cross, and crucified. Someone carrying a cross was someone who was about to die. So when Jesus said, "Whoever desires to come after Me, let him deny himself, and take up his cross, and follow Me" (Mark 8:34), His disciples would have understood what He meant.

> Those who belong to Christ Jesus
> have nailed the **passions** and desires
> of their sinful nature to his cross
> and **crucified** them there.
> GALATIANS 5:24 NLT

Taking up the cross speaks of dying to yourself and wanting God's will more than your own. It doesn't mean your life is ruined when you decide to walk with God. What it does mean is that now you'll have life and have it more abundantly as Jesus promised, because you want God's will more than your own. Jesus said, "Whoever desires to save his life will lose it, but whoever loses his life for My sake and the gospel's will save it" (Mark 8:35).

Are you taking up the cross and following Jesus? Bearing the cross will influence every aspect of your life. The result will be life as it was meant to be lived—in the perfect will of God.

THE LORD'S INVITATION TO HIS PEOPLE

Whoever desires to come after Me,
let him deny himself, and take up his cross,
and follow Me.

JESUS, IN MARK 8:34

WITH GOD IN PRAYER

Answer this question honestly before God: Are you taking up your cross and following Jesus?

MOVE BEYOND A WRONG VIEW
OF CROSS BEARING

What does taking up your cross mean specifically in your life? If you are unsure, ask the Lord to make it clear to you.

Your own reflections...personal application... personal prayer points...

No Greater Gift

Some of the most precious gifts tend not to attract our attention at first. We take a hurried glance and see nothing of significance. But if we go back and take another look, we begin to discover the glory and the wonder of that gift.

So it was with Christ when He came to earth as a helpless baby in a manger: He was the only begotten Son of God. Words cannot completely describe it, as Paul wrote in 2 Corinthians, "Thanks be to God for His indescribable gift!" (9:15). Even God couldn't give a greater gift than He has given. He gave His dearly beloved Son. He sent into the world the One who was with Him from all eternity and then sacrificed Him.

Our Lord Himself spoke of such a sacrificial act in His parable about the vineyard owner. The owner, who had unworthy servants looking after his property, sent his representatives and servants to the vineyard. One after the other was maltreated, even killed. Then the owner thought, "If I send my son, they won't do this to him. Surely they will respect my son. There's nothing beyond this. It's the last act" (see Matthew 21:33–46).

> Every good gift and every **perfect** gift
> is from above, and comes down from the
> **Father of lights**, with whom there
> is no variation or shadow of turning.
>
> JAMES 1:17

Hebrews 1:1 tells us how God sent many servants into the world and to the nation of Israel. God has given the world many outstanding men and women. But He has surpassed them all with the gift of His Son.

This should fill our minds and hearts with astonishment. God has done something that even He Himself cannot exceed. He gave His only Son, His eternal Son, sending Him into the world.

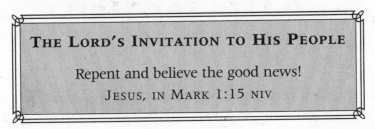

THE LORD'S INVITATION TO HIS PEOPLE

Repent and believe the good news!
JESUS, IN MARK 1:15 NIV

WITH GOD IN PRAYER

Express your thanksgiving to Him for His greatest gift.

MOVE BEYOND TOO LITTLE APPRECIATION FOR GOD'S GREATEST GIFT

What kinds of things are most likely to block you from being thankful for God's gift of His Son?

Your own reflections...personal application... personal prayer points...

Gifts for God

I've discovered how true it is that giving is more blessed than receiving. If you're like me, you can't wait to give your gifts. When you get something for someone, you want to see the joy he or she has in receiving it.

The wise men brought gifts to Jesus—gold, frankincense, and myrrh. What kind of gifts are these for a child? Myrrh, after all, is an embalming element. Why give an embalming element to a baby? I believe these wise men had insight into who Jesus was. They gave Him gold because they recognized it was a proper gift for a king. They gave him frankincense because that's what a high priest used when he went into the temple to represent the people before God. They gave Him myrrh in recognition that this king and high priest would die for the world.

> We have seen His **star** in the East
> and have come to **worship** Him.
> MATTHEW 2:2

What can we give to God? What do you give to God, who has everything? What does God want from us? He wants our lives.

The greatest gift you can give to God is yourself. The greatest gift you can give to God is to step forward into the future and say, *Lord, I give You my life. I give You my talents. I give You my abilities. I give You my dreams. I give You my future. I give You my weaknesses. I offer myself to You. Here's my gift to You.*

Let's be like these wise men and worship Him and give to Him. You'll be glad you did, because you can never outgive God.

THE LORD'S INVITATION TO HIS PEOPLE

Oh come, let us worship and bow down;
let us kneel before the LORD our Maker.

PSALM 95:6

WITH GOD IN PRAYER

In a new and fresh way, fully offer your life to Him. Tell Him, *I give You my talents. I give You my abilities. I give You my dreams. I give You my future. I give You my weaknesses. I offer myself to You.*

MOVE BEYOND HOLDING YOURSELF
BACK FROM GOD

What most often holds you back from fully giving yourself to God? How can you make progress in being more available to Him with all of your life?

Your own reflections...personal application... personal prayer points...

Giving Our Best

A farmer known for his frugality owned a cow that gave birth to two calves. He said to his wife, "I'm going to dedicate one of these calves to the Lord."

Knowing his miserly ways, she was surprised by this. She asked which one he was planning to give to the Lord. "I haven't decided yet," he answered, "but I'll let you know."

A few days went by, and again she asked which calf he was giving to the Lord. "I'm still thinking about it," he told her.

Then one day, one of the calves got sick. Its condition grew worse, until one night the farmer walked up on the porch with the calf draped over his arms. He said to his wife, "Honey, I have bad news. The Lord's calf just died."

Many times we tend to give God what we don't really want ourselves. Think about a typical day. What place do we give to the things of God? Maybe we utter a quick prayer as we roll out of bed or offer some hurried words of thanks over breakfast? Then we rush off to our responsibilities. At the end of the day, we say, "I'll give God these last few minutes as I'm dozing off."

> What can I **offer** the LORD
> for all he has **done** for me?
> PSALM 116:12 NLT

If God is important, why do we give Him our leftovers? God doesn't want our leftovers. God once said to His people,

You have shown contempt by offering defiled sacrifices on my altar.
Then you ask, "How have we defiled the sacrifices?" You defile them by
saying the altar of the LORD deserves no respect. (Malachi 1:7 NLT)

God gave us His best. Let's give Him ours.

THE LORD'S INVITATION TO HIS PEOPLE

Offer right sacrifices,
and put your trust in the LORD.
PSALM 4:5 ESV

WITH GOD IN PRAYER

Praise Him for the truth that He deserves our very best.

MOVE BEYOND GIVING GOD LESS
THAN YOUR BEST

In a practical way today, what does giving God your best actually mean?

Your own reflections...personal application... personal prayer points...

The Smart
Thing to Do

Whose slave are you? Maybe you believe you're your own person, the master of your own destiny. But in reality, each of us yields or gives ourselves to someone or something. We're all slaves of someone or something.

I want to be a slave of God.

> Do you not **know** that to whom
> you present yourselves slaves to
> obey, you are that one's **slaves**
> whom **you** obey, whether of sin
> leading to death, or of obedience
> leading to **righteousness**?
> ROMANS 6:16

The apostle Paul wrote to believers, "Having been set free from sin, and having become slaves of God, you have your fruit to holiness, and the end, everlasting life" (Romans 6:22). This word *slave* is translated from a Greek word that would have been readily understood in that culture. It referred to a slave who had been bought off the auction block and then granted freedom. In other words, the master would purchase that slave and then set him or her free. Slaves who were so thankful to their masters for such a compassionate gesture and wanted to voluntarily serve them would be designated as a bondslave, meaning a voluntary slave.

The grateful slave was not a slave for pay or a slave out of fear, but a slave by choice—a loving servant. That's what Paul said he was, and that's also what we ought to be.

Whose slave are you? You're either a slave of God or you're a slave of sin. The choice is up to you. You can either yield to sin and pay the price and live a miserable life, or you can yield to God, giving Him your gifts, time, and future, and live life to its fullest.

It's the smart thing to do.

THE LORD'S INVITATION TO HIS PEOPLE

Now you are free from your slavery to sin, and you have become slaves to righteous living.... Now you must give yourselves to be slaves to righteous living so that you will become holy.

ROMANS 6:18–19 NLT

WITH GOD IN PRAYER

Come before His throne and make the decision to be His lifelong slave.

MOVE BEYOND THE FOOLISHNESS OF NOT YIELDING TO GOD

What comes to your mind when you think of being God's slave?

Your own reflections...personal application... personal prayer points...

Conformed
or Transformed?

A flock of wild geese was flying south for the winter when one goose looked down and noticed a group of domestic geese by a little pond near a farm. He noticed they had plenty of grain to eat. Life seemed relatively nice for them. So he flew down and hung out with these geese until spring and enjoyed the food there. He decided he would rejoin his flight of geese when they went north again.

When spring came, he heard the wild geese overhead and flew up to join them, but he'd grown a bit fat from all the seed. Flying was difficult, so he decided to spend one more season on the farm and then rejoin the geese on their next winter migration.

When the geese flew south the following fall, the goose flapped his wings a little, but he just kept eating his grain. He'd simply lost interest in rejoining the others.

> This world is fading away, along with **everything** that people crave. But anyone who does what pleases God will live **forever**.
>
> 1 John 2:17 NLT

That's what happens in the subtle process of the world influencing our lives. It isn't necessarily dramatic, nor does it usually happen overnight. It's gradual, causing erosion in our lives as we begin to lower our standards. Soon the things of God become less appealing, and the things of this world become more appealing. After a while, we have no interest in the things of God.

We have a choice: either we'll be conformed to this world, or we'll be transformed by the renewing of our minds. It's one or the other. The only question is, Which will you choose?

THE LORD'S INVITATION TO HIS PEOPLE

Don't copy the behavior and customs of this world, but let God transform you into a new person by changing the way you think. Then you will learn to know God's will for you.

ROMANS 12:2 NLT

WITH GOD IN PRAYER

Let Him know your desire to have Him renew your mind and transform your way of thinking.

MOVE BEYOND CONFORMITY TO THE WORLD

What old ways of thinking do you need to get rid of?

Your own reflections...personal application... personal prayer points...

Destruction in Disguise

One of the first things I remember taking place when I committed my life to Jesus Christ was the erosion of my bitterness and anger. They were replaced by a growing love that I hadn't known before. Years of resentment that had been building up just began to dissolve.

If we claim to be followers of Christ and harbor bitterness or hatred in our hearts toward someone, there's something very wrong with us.

John's meaning was very distinct when he wrote,

> If someone says, "I love God," but hates a Christian brother or sister,
> that person is a liar; for if we don't love people we can see, how can we
> love God, whom we cannot see? (1 John 4:20 NLT)

John was saying that if we have hatred in our hearts toward fellow members of the body of Christ, fellow Christians, there's something wrong in our spiritual lives.

> Beloved, let us **love** one another,
> for love is of God; and everyone who
> loves is **born** of God and knows God.
> 1 John 4:7

Maybe someone has wronged or hurt you. Yet you are to love. You're to forgive. You're not to avenge yourself. Here's why: that bitterness and hatred will do more harm to you than the person to whom you're directing it. It will eat you up inside. It will destroy your life. It will hinder your time of prayer with God. It will hinder your worship. It will, for all practical purposes, act as an obstacle in the relationship God wants to have with you.

There's no room for hatred in the heart of a child of God. There's no room for bitterness. There's no room for prejudice. God wants our love to be honest, and He wants it to be without hypocrisy.

THE LORD'S INVITATION TO HIS PEOPLE

Don't just pretend to love others.
Really love them. Hate what is wrong.
Hold tightly to what is good.
ROMANS 12:9 NLT

WITH GOD IN PRAYER

Thank Him for the purity of His love for you and for setting that as the standard in your relationships with others.

MOVE BEYOND HATRED'S HARM

Do you have any built-up bitterness or anger toward others that needs to be dealt with before God? If so, do this immediately, and discover God's healing and His peace.

Your own reflections...personal application... personal prayer points...

A Work in Progress

I'm an artist. I like to draw and design. Sometimes when I begin a sketch, someone will come along, look over my shoulder, and not see much.

"What is it going to be?" the person asks.

"Just wait."

"I don't like it. I can't tell what it is."

"Just let me finish," I say. "Then I'll gladly show it to you."

Every artist loves to display his finished work. But when it's still a work in progress, the critic doesn't yet see what the artist sees.

That's how we can be with God sometimes. "Hey, Lord, what are You doing here? What's going on?"

> He has made everything beautiful in its **time**. Also He has put **eternity** in their hearts, except that no one can **find** out the work that **God** does from beginning to end.
>
> ECCLESIASTES 3:11

You, too, are a work in progress. God is doing a work in your life. When it's done, He'll show you. If it isn't done yet, be patient. God sees the end from the beginning. We see only what's happening now, but God sees what He'll do in the future. That's important to remember.

As God told the exiled nation of Israel,

I know the plans I have for you.... They are plans for good and not for disaster, to give you a future and a hope. (Jeremiah 29:11 NLT)

For Israel, God's plan meant that they would be in Babylon for a while; ultimately, however, God would get them out.

For us, only time will tell the day-to-day specifics of what God will do with us and for us. Whatever it is, it will be good, because God is in control of it.

God has a plan in mind for you. And as I've said many times, the word *oops* isn't in God's vocabulary. So rejoice. God doesn't make mistakes. He doesn't forget about what He's doing. And He doesn't forget about you.

THE LORD'S INVITATION TO HIS PEOPLE

Let patience have its perfect work, that you may be perfect and complete, lacking nothing.

JAMES 1:4

WITH GOD IN PRAYER

Give Him thanks for the perfect future He has planned for you.

MOVE BEYOND IMPATIENCE WITH GOD

What convinces you that God's timing can be fully trusted? If there's something that's blocking you from that kind of trust in Him, confess that to Him, repent of it...and move forward into His perfect will for your future.

Your own reflections...personal application... personal prayer points...

TOPIC INDEX

SCRIPTURE INDEX